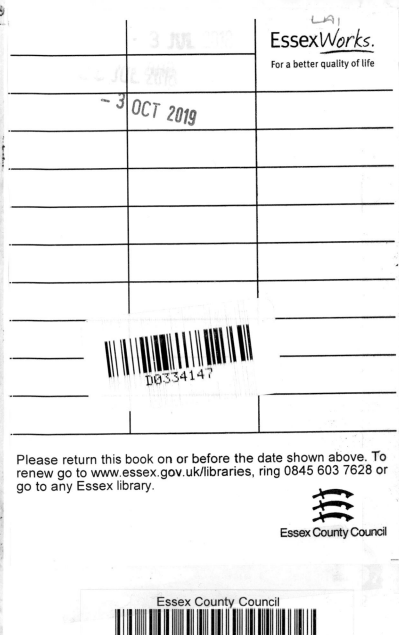

Credits

Footprint credits
Editorial: Nicola Gibbs
Maps: Kevin Feeney
Proofreader: Sophie Jones
Cover: Pepi Bluck

Publisher: Patrick Dawson
Managing Editor: Felicity Laughton
Advertising: Elizabeth Taylor
Sales and marketing: Kirsty Holmes

Photography credits
Front cover: Sebastian Feszler/
Dreamstime.com
Back cover: Stewart Smith Photography/
Shutterstock

Printed in Great Britain by CPI Antony Rowe,
Chippenham, Wiltshire

MIX
Paper from
responsible sources
FSC® C013604
www.fsc.org

Contains Ordnance Survey data
© Crown copyright and database
right 2013

Publishing information
Footprint *Focus Lake District, Cumbria
& Northumberland*
1st edition
© Footprint Handbooks Ltd
April 2013

ISBN: 978 1 909268 15 9
CIP DATA: A catalogue record for this book
is available from the British Library

® Footprint Handbooks and the Footprint
mark are a registered trademark of Footprint
Handbooks Ltd

Published by Footprint
6 Riverside Court
Lower Bristol Road
Bath BA2 3DZ, UK
T +44 (0)1225 469141
F +44 (0)1225 469461
footprinttravelguides.com

Distributed in the USA by Globe Pequot Press,
Guilford, Connecticut

The content of Footprint *Focus Lake District,
Cumbria & Northumberland* has been updated
from Footprint's *England Handbook* which
was researched and written by Charlie
Godfrey-Faussett.

Contents

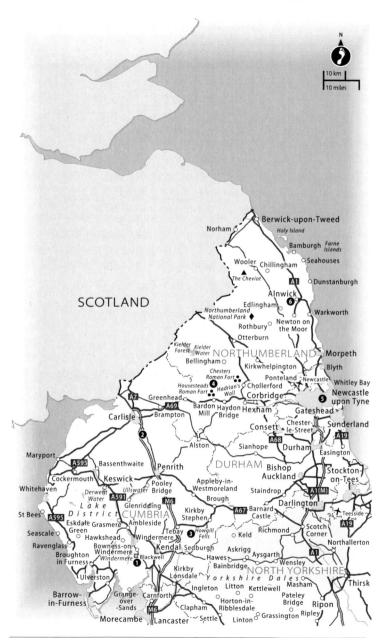

First impressions of the sparsely populated far north of England are likely to involve its big landscape and bad weather. Spread wide under changeable skies, the north is hard-bitten but open-hearted. Largely, it has yet to resort to the more cynical trappings of commercialized mass tourism. Sadly, though, that's no longer entirely true of its most popular destination, the Lake District. This mountainous little bit of Cumbria off the M6 has been pulling in the punters for centuries, not without good reason. Here, the landscape celebrated by the Romantic poets still stirs the soul, but the roads winding through it are often terribly overcrowded. The rest of Cumbria offers more peaceful touring, hiking and strolling, especially around the rivers Eden and Lune.

To the north, Carlisle broods on its troubled history close to the Scottish border and makes a good base for exploration of the country's longest Roman landmark, Hadrian's Wall. At the other end of the wall, the city of Newcastle upon Tyne is the largest in the north and has reinvented itself as a happening European cultural centre, with close ferry links to Scandinavia. To its south, Durham rests on its laurels as the 'land of the Prince Bishops', boasting one of the most spectacular pieces of old architecture in the UK: its hilltop Norman cathedral.

Further north than all these, one of the least spoiled or hyped counties in England, Northumberland seems determined to keep it that way. Although it is sometimes chilly and bleak, it also rains less often here than almost anywhere else. Mile upon mile of deserted beaches are holiday heaven around Alnwick, while the crowds still flock to the Holy Island of Lindisfarne, near to the doughty border town of Berwick-upon-Tweed. It sits on the northern edge of the Northumberland National Park – a big treat for serious ramblers.

Planning your trip

Best time to visit England

The weather in England is notoriously unpredictable. It is generally better between May and September, although it can be gloriously hot in April and cold and damp in August. The west of the country is milder and wetter than the east, whilst northern and mountainous areas are usually the coldest.

Transport in England

Compared to the rest of Western Europe, public transport in England is expensive and can be unreliable. Rail tickets, in particular, should be booked well in advance to avoid paying extortionate prices. Coach travel is cheaper but slower, and can be hampered by traffic problems particularly around London, Manchester and Birmingham. If you plan to spend much time in rural areas, it may be worth hiring a car, especially if you are travelling as a couple or group. A useful website for all national public transport information is **Traveline** ① *T0871-200 2233, www.traveline.info.*

Air
England is a small country and air travel isn't necessary to get around. However, with traffic a problem around the cities, some of the cheap fares offered by budget airlines may be very attractive. There are good connections between **London** and all the regional airports, although travel from region to region without coming through London is more difficult and expensive. Bear in mind the time and money it will take you to get to the airport (including check-in times) when deciding whether flying is really going to be a better deal.

Airport information National Express operates a frequent service between London's main airports. **London Heathrow Airport** ① *16 miles west of London between junctions 3 and 4 on the M4, T0844-335 1801, www.heathrowairport.com,* is the world's busiest international airport and it has five terminals, so when leaving London, it's important to check which terminal to go to before setting out for the airport. To get into central London, the cheapest option is the London Underground Piccadilly Line (50 minutes). The fastest option is **Heathrow Express** ① *T0845-6001515, www.heathrowexpress.com,* taking 15-20 minutes. There is a train service **Heathrow Connect** ① *Heathrow T0845-748 4950, www.heathrowconnect.com,* which takes 25 minutes. Coaches to destinations all over the country are run by **National Express** ① *T0871-781 8181, www.nationalexpress.com.* There are also buses to Oxford (www.oxfordbus.co.uk), to Reading for trains to Bristol and southwest England (www.railair.com), to Watford for trains to the north of England (www.greenline.co.uk) and to West London (www.tfl.gov.uk). A taxi to central London takes one hour and costs £45-70.

    London Gatwick Airport ① *28 miles south of London, off junction 9 on the M23, T0844-892 03222, www.gatwickairport.com,* has two terminals, North and South, with all the usual facilities. To central London, there is the **Gatwick Express** ① *T0845-850 1530,*

Don't miss...

www.gatwickexpress.com, from £17.75 single online, which takes 30 minutes. Thameslink rail services run from King's Cross, Farringdon, Blackfriars and London Bridge stations. Contact **National Rail Enquiries** (T0845-748 4950, www.nationalrail.co.uk) for further information. **EasyBus** (www.easybus.co.uk) is the cheapest option, with prices starting at £9.99 for a single, taking just over an hour. A taxi takes a similar time and costs from around £60.

London City Airport ① *Royal Dock, 6 miles (15 mins' drive) east of the City of London, T020-7646 0000, www.londoncityairport.com.* Take the **Docklands Light Railway** (DLR) to Canning Town (seven minutes) for the **Jubilee line** or a connecting shuttle bus service. A taxi into central London will cost around £35.

London Luton Airport ① *30 miles north of central London, 2 miles off the M1 at junction 10, southeast of Luton, Beds, T01582-405100, www.london-luton.co.uk.* Regular **First Capital Connect** trains run to central London; a free shuttle bus service operates between the airport terminal and the station. **Green Line** (www.greenline.co.uk) coaches run to central London, as does **easyBus** (www.easybus.co.uk). **National Express** (www.nationalexpress.com) operates coaches to many destinations. A taxi takes 50 minutes, costing from £70.

Stansted Airport ① *35 miles northeast of London (near Cambridge) by junction 8 of the M11, T0844-335 1803, www.stanstedairport.com.* **Stansted Express** (T0845-600 7245, www.stanstedexpress.com) runs trains to London's Liverpool Street Station (45 minutes, £22.50 single). **EasyBus** (www.easybus.co.uk, from £2), **Terravision** (www.terravision.eu, £9) and **National Express** (www.nationalexpress.com, from £8.50) run to central London (55 minutes to East London, 1 hour 30 minutes to Victoria). A taxi to central London takes around an hour to 1 hour 30 minutes, depending on traffic, and costs around £99.

Manchester International Airport ① *junction 5 of the M56, T0871-271 0711, www.manchesterairport.co.uk.* The airport is well served by public transport, with trains to and from Manchester Piccadilly as well as direct and connecting services from all over the north of England. **National Express** (www.nationalexpress.com) runs routes covering the whole of the UK. A taxi into the city centre should cost around £20.

Birmingham International Airport (BHX) ① *8 miles east of the city centre at junction 6 on the M42, T0871-222 0072, www.birminghamairport.co.uk.* A taxi into the centre should cost from £25. Several trains per hour run the free 10-minute Air-Rail Link to Birmingham International Station, and other connections across England and Wales can be made by rail or coach, with **National Express** (www.nationalexpress.com).

Rail

National Rail Enquiries ① *T08457-484950, www.nationalrail.co.uk*, are quick and courteous with information on rail services and fares but not always accurate, so double check. They can't book tickets but will provide you with the relevant telephone number. The website, www.thetrainline.co.uk, also shows prices clearly.

Railcards There are a variety of railcards which give discounts on fares for certain groups. Cards are valid for one year and most are available from main stations. You need two passport photos and proof of age or status. A Young Person's Railcard is for those aged 16-25 or full-time students aged 26+ in the UK. Costs £28 for one year and gives 33% discount on most train tickets and some other services (www.16-25railcard.co.uk). A Senior Citizen's Railcard is for those aged over 60, is the same price and offers the same discounts as a Young Person's Railcard (www.senior-railcard.co.uk). A Disabled Person's Railcard costs £20 and gives 33% discount to a disabled person and one other. Pick up an application form from stations and send it to Disabled Person's Railcard Office, PO Box 11631, Laurencekirk AB30 9AA. It may take up to 10 working days to be delivered, so apply in advance (www.disabledpersons-railcard.co.uk). A Family & Friends Railcard costs £28 and gives 33% discount on most tickets for up to four adults travelling together, and 60% discount for up to four children. It's available to buy online as well as in most stations.

Road

Bus and coach Travelling by bus takes longer than the train but is much cheaper. Road links between cities and major towns in England are excellent, but far less frequent in more remote rural areas, and a number of companies offer express coach services day and night. The main operator is **National Express** ① *T08717-818178, www.national express.com*, which has a nationwide network with over 1000 destinations. Tickets can be bought at bus stations, from a huge number of agents throughout the country or online. Sample return fares if booked in advance: London to Manchester (4 hours 35 minutes) £28, London to Cambridge (2 hours 30 mins) £12. **Megabus** ① *T0900-160 0 900 (61p a min from BT landlines, calls from other networks may be higher), http://megabus.com*, is a cheaper alternative with a more limited service.

Full-time students, those aged under 25 or over 60 or those registered disabled, can buy a coach card for £10 which is valid for one year and gets you a 30% discount on all fares. Children normally travel for half price, but with a **Family Card** costing £16, two children travel free with two adults. Available to overseas passport holders, the **Brit Xplorer Pass** offers unlimited travel on all National Express buses. Passes cost from £79 for seven days, £139 for 14 days and £219 for its month-long **Rolling Stone Pass**. They can be bought from major airports and bus terminals.

Car Travelling with your own private transport is the ideal way to explore the country, particularly in areas with limited public transport. This allows you to cover a lot of ground in a short space of time and to reach remote places. The main disadvantages are rising fuel costs, parking and traffic congestion. The latter is particularly heavy on the M25 which encircles London, the M6 around Birmingham and the M62 around Manchester. The M4 and M5 motorways to the West Country can also become choked at weekends and bank holidays and the roads in Cornwall often resemble a glorified car park during the summer.

Motoring organizations can help with route planning, traffic advice, insurance and breakdown cover. The two main ones are: the **Automobile Association (AA)** ① *T0800-085 2721, emergency number T0800-887766, www.theaa.com*, which offers a year's breakdown cover starting at £38, and the **Royal Automobile Club (RAC)** ① *T0844-273 4341, emergency number T08000-828282, www.rac.co.uk*, which has a year's breakdown cover starting at £31.99. Both have cover for emergency assistance. You can still call the emergency numbers if you're not a member, but you'll have to a pay a large fee.

Vehicle hire
Car hire is expensive and the minimum you can expect to pay is around £100 per week for a small car. Always check and compare conditions, such as mileage limitations, excess payable in the case of an accident, etc. Small, local hire companies often offer better deals than the larger multinationals. Most companies prefer payment with a credit card – some insist on it – otherwise you'll have to leave a large deposit (£100 or more). You need to have had a full driver's licence for at least a year and to be aged between 21 (25 for some companies) and 70.

Bicycle
Cycling is a pleasant if slightly hazardous way to see the country. Although conditions for cyclists are improving, with a growing network of cycle lanes in cities, most other roads do not have designated cycle paths, and cyclists are not allowed on motorways. You can load your bike onto trains, though some restrictions apply during rush hour. See the website www.ctc.org.uk for information on routes, restrictions and facilities.

Where to stay in England

Accommodation can mean anything from being pampered to within an inch of your life in a country house spa hotel to glamping in a yurt. If you have the money, then the sky is very much the limit in terms of sheer splendour and excess. We have tried to give as broad a selection as possible to cater for all tastes and budgets, with a bias towards those that offer that little bit extra in terms of character.

If you can't find what you're after, or if someone else has beaten you to the draw, then the tourist information centres (TICs) will help find accommodation for you. Some offices charge a small fee (usually £1) for booking a room, while others ask you to pay a deposit of 10% which is deducted from your first night's bill. Details of town and city TICs are given throughout the guide.

Accommodation will be your greatest expense, particularly if you are travelling on your own. Single rooms are in short supply and many places are reluctant to let a double room to one person, even when they're not busy. Single rooms typically cost around 75% of the price of a double room, although some establishments do not charge single supplements.

Hotels, guesthouses and B&Bs
Area tourist boards publish accommodation lists that include campsites, hostels, self-catering accommodation, hotels, guesthouses and bed and breakfasts (B&Bs). Places participating in the VisitEngland system will have a plaque displayed outside which shows their grading, determined by a number of stars ranging from one to five. These

Price codes

Where to stay

£££££ over £160   £££ £90-160

££ £50-90   £ under £50

Prices include taxes and service charge, but not meals. They are based on a one-night stay in a double room in high season.

Restaurants

£££ over £30   ££ £15-30   £ under £15

Prices refer to the cost of a two-course meal for one person, without a drink.

reflect the level of facilities, as well as the quality of hospitality and service. However, do not assume that a B&B, guesthouse or hotel is no good because it is not listed by the tourist board. They simply don't want to pay to be included in the system, and some of them may offer better value.

Hotels At the top end of the scale there are some fabulously luxurious hotels, some in beautiful locations. Some are converted mansions or castles, and offer a chance to enjoy a taste of aristocratic grandeur and style. At the lower end of the scale, there is often little to choose between cheaper hotels and guesthouses or B&Bs. The latter often offer higher standards of comfort and a more personal service, but many smaller hotels are really just guesthouses, and are often family run and every bit as friendly. Rooms in most mid-range to expensive hotels almost always have bathrooms en suite. Many upmarket hotels offer excellent room-only deals in the low season. An efficient last-minute hotel booking service is www.laterooms.com, which specializes in weekend breaks. Also note that many hotels offer cheaper rates for online booking through agencies such as www.lastminute.com.

Guesthouses Guesthouses are often large, converted family homes with up to five or six rooms. They tend to be slightly more expensive than B&Bs, charging between £30 and £50 per person per night, and though they are often less personal, usually provide better facilities, such as en suite bathroom, TV in each room, free Wi-Fi and private parking. Many guesthouses offer evening meals, though this may have to be requested in advance.

Bed and breakfasts (B&Bs) B&Bs usually provide the cheapest private accommodation. At the bottom end of the scale you can get a bedroom in a private house, a shared bathroom and a huge cooked breakfast from around £25 per person per night. Small B&Bs may only have one or two rooms to let, so it's important to book in advance during the summer season. More upmarket B&Bs, some in handsome period houses, have en suite bathrooms, free Wi-Fi and TVs in each room and usually charge from £35 per person per night.

Hostels

For those travelling on a tight budget, there is a network of hostels offering cheap accommodation in major cities, national parks and other areas of beauty, run by the **Youth Hostel Association (YHA)** ① *T01629-592600, or customer services T0800-019 1700,*

+44-1629-592700 from outside the UK, www.yha.org.uk. Membership costs from £14.35 a year and a bed in a dormitory costs from £15 to £25 a night. They offer bunk-bed accommodation in single-sex dormitories or smaller rooms, as well as family rooms, kitchen and laundry facilities. Though some rural hostels are still strict on discipline and impose a 2300 curfew, those in larger towns and cities tend to be more relaxed and doors are closed as late as 0200. Some larger hostels provide breakfasts for around £2.50 and three-course evening meals for £4-5. You should always phone ahead, as many hostels are closed during the day and phone numbers are listed in this guide. Advance booking is recommended at all times, particularly from May to September and on public holidays. Many hostels are closed during the winter. Youth hostel members are entitled to various discounts, including tourist attractions and travel. The YHA also offer budget self-catering bunkhouses with mostly dorm accommodation and some family rooms, which are in more rural locations. Camping barns, camping pods and camping are other options offered by the YHA; see the website for details.

Details of most independent hostels can be found in the *Independent Hostel Guide* (T01629-580427, www.independenthostelguide.co.uk). Independent hostels tend to be more laid-back, with fewer rules and no curfew, and no membership is required. They all have dorms, hot showers and self-catering kitchens, and some have family and double rooms. Some include continental breakfast, or offer cheap breakfasts.

Self-catering accommodation
There are lots of different types of accommodation to choose from, to suit all budgets, ranging from luxury lodges, castles and lighthouses to basic cottages. Expect to pay at least £200-400 per week for a two-bedroom cottage in the winter, rising to £400-1000 in the high season, or more if it's a particularly nice place. A good source of information on self-catering accommodation is the **VisitEngland** website, www.visitengland.com, and its *VisitEngland Self-catering 2013* guide, which lists many properties and is available to buy from any tourist office and many bookshops, but there are also dozens of excellent websites to browse. Amongst the best websites are: www.cottages4you.co.uk, www.ruralretreats.co.uk and www.ownersdirect.co.uk. If you want to tickle a trout or feed a pet lamb, **Farm Stay UK** (www.farmstay.co.uk) offers over a thousand good value rural places to stay around England, all clearly listed on a clickable map.

More interesting places to stay are offered by the **Landmark Trust** ① *T01628-825925, www.landmarktrust.org.uk*, who rent out renovated historic landmark buildings, from atmospheric castles to cottages, and the **National Trust** ① *T0844-800 2070, www.national trustcottages.co.uk*, who provide a wide variety of different accommodation on their estates. A reputable agent for self-catering cottages is **English Country Cottages** ① *T0845-268 0785, www.english-country-cottages.co.uk.*

Campsites
Campsites vary greatly in quality and level of facilities. Some sites are only open from April to October. See the following sites: www.pitchup.com; www.coolcamping.com, good for finding characterful sites that allow campfires; www.ukcampsite.co.uk, which is the most comprehensive service with thousands of sites, many with pictures and reviews from punters; and www.campingandcaravanningclub.co.uk. The **Forestry Commission** have campsites on their wooded estates, see www.campingintheforest.com.

Food and drink in England

Food

Only 30 years ago few would have thought to come to England for haute cuisine. Since the 1980s, though, the English have been determinedly shrugging off their reputation for over-boiled cabbage and watery beef. Now cookery shows such as *Masterchef* are the most popular on TV after the soaps, and thanks in part to the wave of celebrity chefs they have created, you can expect a generally high standard of competence in restaurant kitchens. Pub food has also been transformed in recent years, and now many of them offer ambitious lunchtime and supper menus in so-called gastro pubs.

Most parts of the country still boast regional specialities and thanks to the diversity of ethnic communities, restaurants offer food from all over the world. Enjoy Chinatowns and diverse styles of Asian cooking in the cities, or cosy up next to a roaring log fire in the Lake District to sample some home-cooked specialities such as Lancashire hotpot, black pudding, Pan Haggerty (made with potatoes, onions and cheese), Bakewell pudding, York hams and mild Cheshire cheese. The Sunday roast is a fine English tradition, best served with Yorkshire puddings, while Afternoon Tea of jam and scones is ever popular.

The biggest problem with eating out is the limited serving hours in some pubs and hotels, particularly in more remote locations. Some establishments only serve food 1200-1430 for lunch and 1830-2130 for supper. In small places especially, it can be difficult finding food outside these enforced times. Restaurants, fast-food outlets and the many chic bistros and café-bars, which can be found not only in the main cities but increasingly in smaller towns, often serve food all day till 2100 or later. The latter often offer very good value and above-average quality fare.

Drink

Drinking is a national hobby and sometimes a dangerous one at that. **Real ale** – flat, brown beer known as bitter, made with hops – is the national drink, but now struggles to maintain its market share in the face of fierce competition from continental lagers and alcopops. Many small independent breweries are still up and running though, as well as microbreweries attached to individual pubs, which produce far superior ales. Local specialities include the creamy headed local bitters – John Smith and Theakstons – and the potent Newcastle Brown Ale. In many pubs the basic ales are chilled under gas pressure like lagers, but the best ales, such as those from the independents, are 'real ales', still fermenting in the cask and served cool but not chilled (around 12°C) under natural pressure from a handpump, electric pump or air pressure fount. **Cider** (fermented apple juice) is also experiencing a resurgence of interest and is a speciality of Somerset. English **wine** is also proving surprisingly resilient: generally it compares favourably with German varieties and many vineyards now offer continental-style sampling sessions.

The **pub** is still traditional place to enjoy a drink: the best are usually freehouses (not tied to a brewery) and feature real log fires in winter, flower-filled gardens for the summer (even in cities occasionally) and most importantly, thriving local custom. Many also offer characterful accommodation and restaurants serving high-quality fare. Pubs are prey to the same market forces as any other business, though, and many a delightful local has succumbed to exorbitant property prices or to the bland makeover favoured by the large chains. In 2012, pubs were closing at the rate of 12 a week due to the recession.

Essentials A-Z

Accident and emergency
For police, fire brigade, ambulance and, in certain areas, mountain rescue or coastguard, T999 or T112.

Disabled travellers
Wheelchair users, and blind or partially sighted people are automatically given 34-50% discount on train fares, and those with other disabilities are eligible for the Disabled Person's Railcard, which costs £20 per year and gives a third off most tickets. If you will need assistance at a railway station, call the train company that manages the station you're starting your journey from 24 hrs in advance. Disabled UK residents can apply to their local councils for a concessionary bus pass. National Express have a helpline for disabled passengers, T08717-818179, to plan journeys and arrange assistance. They also sell a discount coach card for £10 for people with disabilities.

The English Tourist Board website, www.visitengland.com, has information on the National Accessible Scheme (NAS) logos to help disabled travellers find the right accommodation for their needs, as well as details of walks that are possible with wheelchairs and the Shopmobility scheme. Many local tourist offices offer accessibility details for their area.

Useful organizations include:
Radar, T020-7250 3222, www.radar.org.uk. A good source of advice and information. It produces an annual National Key Scheme Guide and key for gaining access to over 9000 toilet facilities across the UK.
Tourism for all, T0845-124 9971, www.holidaycare.org.uk, www.tourismfor all.org.uk. An excellent source of information about travel and for identifying accessible accommodation in the UK.

Electricity
The current in Britain is 240V AC. Plugs have 3 square pins and adapters are widely available.

Health
For minor accidents go to the nearest casualty department or an Accident and Emergency (A&E) Unit at a hospital. For other enquiries phone NHS Direct 24 hrs (T0845-4647) or visit an NHS walk-in centre. See also individual town and city directories throughout the book for details of local medical services.

Money → *For up-to-date exchange rates, see www.xe.com.*
The British currency is the pound sterling (£), divided into 100 pence (p). Coins come in denominations of 1p, 2p, 5p, 10p, 20p, 50p, £1 and £2. Banknotes come in denominations of £5, £10, £20 and £50. The last of these is not widely used and may be difficult to change.

Banks and bureaux de change
Banks tend to offer similar exchange rates and are usually the best places to change money and cheques. Outside banking hours you'll have to use a bureau de change, which can be easily found at the airports and train stations and in larger cities. **Thomas Cook** and other major travel agents also operate bureaux de change with reasonable rates. Avoid changing money or cheques in hotels, as the rates are usually poor. Main post offices and branches of **Marks and Spencer** will change cash without charging commission.

Credit cards and ATMs
Most hotels, shops and restaurants accept the major credit cards though some places may charge for using them. Some smaller establishments such as B&Bs may only accept cash.

Currency cards

If you don't want to carry lots of cash, prepaid currency cards allow you to preload money from your bank account, fixed at the day's exchange rate. They look like a credit or debit card and are issued by specialist money changing companies, such as **Travelex** and **Caxton FX**. You can top up and check your balance by phone, online and sometimes by text.

Money transfers

If you need money urgently, the quickest way to have it sent to you is to have it wired to the nearest bank via **Western Union**, T0800-833833, www.westernunion.co.uk, or **MoneyGram**, www.moneygram.com. The Post Office can also arrange a MoneyGram transfer. Charges are on a sliding scale; so it will cost proportionately less to wire out more money. Money can also be wired by **Thomas Cook**, www.thomasexchangeglobal.co.uk, or transferred via a bank draft, but this can take up to a week.

Taxes

Most goods are subject to a Value Added Tax (VAT) of 20%, with the major exception of food and books. VAT is usually already included in the advertised price of goods. Visitors from non-EU countries can save money through shopping at places that offer Tax Free Shopping (also known as the Retail Export Scheme), which allows a refund of VAT on goods that will be taken out of the country. Note that not all shops participate in the scheme and that VAT cannot be reclaimed on hotel bills or other services.

Cost of travelling

England can be an expensive place to visit, and London and the south in particular can eat heavily into your budget. There is budget accommodation available, however, and backpackers will be able to keep their costs down. Fuel is a major expense and won't just cost an arm and a leg but also the limbs of all remaining family members, and public transport – particularly rail travel if not booked in advance – can also be pricey, especially for families. Accommodation and restaurant prices also tend to be higher in more popular destinations and during the busy summer months.

The minimum daily budget required, if you're staying in hostels or camping, cycling or hitching (not recommended), and cooking your own meals, will be around £30 per person per day. If you start using public transport and eating out occasionally that will rise to around £35-40. Those staying in slightly more upmarket B&Bs or guesthouses, eating out every evening at pubs or modest restaurants and visiting tourist attractions can expect to pay around £60 per day. If you also want to hire a car and eat well, then costs will rise considerably to at least £75-80 per person per day. Single travellers will have to pay more than half the cost of a double room, and should budget on spending around 60-70% of what a couple would spend.

Opening hours

Businesses are usually open Mon-Sat 0900-1700. In towns and cities, as well as villages in holiday areas, many shops open on a Sun but they will open later and close earlier. For banks, see above. For TIC opening hours, see the tourist information sections in the relevant cities, towns and villages in the text.

Post

Most post offices are open Mon-Fri 0900 to 1730 and Sat 0900-1230 or 1300. Smaller sub-post offices are closed for an hour at lunch (1300-1400) and many of them operate out of a shop. Stamps can be bought at post offices, but also from many shops. A 1st-class letter weighing up to 100 g to anywhere in the UK costs 60p (a large letter over 240 mm by 165 mm is 90p) and should arrive the following day, while 2nd-class letters weighing up to 100 g cost 50p (69p) and take between 2-4 days. For more information about Royal Mail postal services, call T08457-740740, or visit www.royalmail.com.

Safety

Generally speaking, England is a safe place to visit. English cities have their fair share of crime, but much of it is drug-related and confined to the more deprived peripheral areas. Trust your instincts, and if in doubt, take a taxi.

Telephone → *Country code +44.*
Useful numbers: operator T100; international operator T155; directory enquiries T192; overseas directory enquiries T153.
Most public payphones are operated by British Telecom (**BT**) and can be found in towns and cities, though less so in rural areas. Numbers of public phone booths have declined in recent years due to the ubiquity of the mobile phone, so don't rely on being able to find a payphone wherever you go. Calls from BT payphones cost a minimum of 60p, for which you get 30 mins for a local or national call. Calls to non-geographic numbers (eg 0845), mobile phones and others may cost more. Payphones take either coins (10p, 20p, 50p and £1), 50c, 1 or 2 euro coins, credit cards or BT Chargecards, which are available at newsagents and post offices displaying the BT logo. These cards come in denominations of £2, £3, £5 and £10. Some payphones also have facilities for internet, text messaging and emailing.

For most countries (including Europe, USA and Canada) calls are cheapest Mon-Fri between 1800 and 0800 and all day Sat-Sun. For Australia and New Zealand it's cheapest to call from 1430-1930 and from 2400-0700 every day. However, the cheapest ways to call abroad from England is not via a standard UK landline provider. Calls are free

using **Skype** on the internet, or you can route calls from your phone through the internet with **JaJah** (www.jajah.com) or from a mobile using **Rebtel**. Many phone companies offer discounted call rates by calling their access number prior to dialling the number you want, including www.dialabroad.co.uk and www.simply-call.com.

Area codes are not needed if calling from within the same area. Any number prefixed by 0800 or 0500 is free to the caller; 08457 numbers are charged at local rates and 08705 numbers at the national rate.

Time

Greenwich Mean Time (GMT) is used from late Oct to late Mar, after which time the clocks go forward 1 hr to British Summer Time (BST).

Tipping

Tipping in England is at the customer's discretion. In a restaurant you should leave a tip of 10-15% if you are satisfied with the service. If the bill already includes a service charge, which is likely if you are in a large group, you needn't add a further tip. Tipping is not normal in pubs or bars. Taxi drivers may expect a tip for longer journeys, usually around 10%.

Tourist information

Tourist information centres (TICs) can be found in most towns. Their addresses, phone numbers and opening hours are listed in the relevant sections of this book. Opening hours vary depending on the time of year, and many of the smaller offices are closed or have limited opening hours during the winter months. All tourist offices provide information on accommodation, public transport, local attractions and restaurants, as well as selling books, local guides, maps and souvenirs. Many also have free street plans and leaflets describing local walks. They can also book accommodation for a small fee.

Museums, galleries and historic houses

Over 300 stately homes, gardens and countryside areas, are cared for by the **National Trust** (**NT**), T0844-800 1895, www.nationaltrust.org.uk. If you're going to be visiting several sights during your stay, then it's worth taking annual membership, which costs £53, £25 if you're aged under 26 and £70 for a family, giving free access to all National Trust properties. A similar organization is **English Heritage** (**EH**), T0870-333 1181, www.english-heritage.org.uk, which manages hundreds of ancient monuments and other sights around England, including Stonehenge, and focuses on restoration and preservation. Membership includes free admission to sites, and advance information on events, and costs £47 per adult to £82 per couple, under-19s free. **Natural England**, T0845-600 3078, www.naturalengland.org.uk, is concerned with restoring and conserving the English countryside, and can give municipal information on walks and events in the countryside.

Many other historic buildings are owned by local authorities, and admission is cheap, or in many cases free. Most municipal art galleries and museums are free, as well as most state-owned museums, particularly those in London and other large cities. Most fee-paying attractions give a discount or concession for senior citizens, the unemployed, full-time students and children under 16 (those under 5 are admitted free in most places). Proof of age or status must be shown.

Finding out more

The best way of finding out more information is to contact VisitEngland (aka the English Tourist Board), www.visitengland.com. Alternatively, you can contact VisitBritain, the organization responsible for tourism. Both organizations can provide a wealth of free literature and information such as maps, city guides and accommodation brochures. Travellers with special needs should also contact VisitEngland or their nearest VisitBritain office. If you want more detailed information on a particular area, contact the specific tourist boards; see in the main text for details.

Visas and immigration

Visa regulations are subject to change, so it is essential to check with your local British embassy, high commission or consulate before leaving home. Citizens of all European countries – except Albania, Bosnia Herzegovina, Kosovo, Macedonia, Moldova, Turkey, Serbia and all former Soviet republics (other than the Baltic states) – require only a passport to enter Britain and can generally stay for up to 3 months. Citizens of Australia, Canada, New Zealand, South Africa or the USA can stay for up to 6 months, providing they have a return ticket and sufficient funds to cover their stay. Citizens of most other countries require a visa from the commission or consular office in the country of application.

The UK Border Agency, www.ukba. homeoffice.gov.uk, is responsible for UK immigration matters and its website is a good place to start for anyone hoping visit, work, study or emigrate to the UK. For visa extensions also contact the UK Border Agency via the website. Citizens of Australia, Canada, New Zealand, South Africa or the USA wishing to stay longer than 6 months will need an Entry Clearance Certificate from the British High Commission in their country. For more details, contact your nearest British embassy, consulate or high commission, or the Foreign and Commonwealth Office in London.

Weights and measures

Imperial and metric systems are both in use. Distances on roads are measured in miles and yards, drinks poured in pints and gills, but generally, the metric system is used elsewhere.

Contents

Footprint features

Lake District, Cumbria & Northumberland

Cumbria and the Lake District

The north by northwestern corner of England comes as quite a surprise. Cumbria embraces the wildest and most spectacular scenery in England. The M6 motorway slices through on its way to Glasgow and even traffic hurtling along this high road gets a taste of the region's bleak beauty. Rising suddenly from sea level to about 3000 ft, the Lake District National Park is no more than 100 miles in circumference but contains 64 lakes, brooded over by some 200 mountains over 2000 ft. Windermere is the largest, most accessible and most famous of the lakes, surrounded by a gentle landscape. Lonely Wastwater is the most extreme, and then there's quiet Ullswater, breezy Bassenthwaite, picturesque Derwentwater and glassy Coniston Water among smaller but equally appealing tarns.

The Lake District may be the most attractive and popular of England's national parks, but unfortunately it knows it only too well. Motorists have been jamming up the narrow mountain roads since the 1920s to spend their holidays here, and environmentalists have had their work cut out trying to balance the conflicting demands of visitors, locals and the natural environment. Large tracts are now in the care of the National Trust, and the region retains the beauty, if not the solitude, that so captivated the Wordsworths 200 years ago.

To the east of the M6, lonelier fells roll off towards County Durham, studded by sturdy pockets of civilization: small market towns such as Sedbergh, Kirkby Stephen and Appleby-in-Westmorland. Westmorland was the old county that bordered Lancashire until the 1970s, but its name lives on throughout the southern part of the new region, providing wonderful walking country that's usually soft underfoot. Cumberland, its northern neighbour, also included the mining communities on the coast and the border country up to Hadrian's Wall and Carlisle, now the county town of Cumbria.

Arriving in Cumbria and the Lake District

Getting there

By road Only too accessible by car from the M6 motorway, most traffic from the south uses Junction 36 (five hours' drive from London) and the dual carriageway A590 for Barrow-in-Furness to reach the Lakes. As the A591 the same road bypasses Kendal after 6 miles (which can also be reached on the winding A684 from Junction 37), and reaches **Windermere**, 7 miles from Kendal. From Windermere, the centre of the Lake District, the lovely A592 runs north over Kirkstone Pass to **Patterdale**, beside Ullswater and finally reaching **Penrith** (26 miles); and south down the eastern shore of Lake Windermere to **Newby Bridge** (9 miles) where it joins the A590 on its way to **Ulverston**, **Barrow-in-Furness** and the **Cumbrian Coast**. From Windermere again, the A591 continues northwest along the northeastern shore of the lake to **Ambleside** (4 miles), past Rydal Water to **Grasmere** (8 miles) and on past Thirlmere to **Keswick** (25 miles). From Ambleside, the A593 heads southwest to **Coniston Water** (10 miles) and **Broughton-in-Furness** (19 miles). Three busy branch roads within 5 miles of Ambleside head south to **Hawkshead**, north to **Langdale**, and west over the steep and narrow Wrynose and Hardknott Passes to **Eskdale**, **Wastwater**, and **Ravenglass** on the Cumbrian Coast. The **Northern Lakes** are most easily reached from Penrith and Junction 40 on the M6, from where the dual-carriageway A66 runs the 17 miles to **Keswick**. From Keswick, the A66 continues to **Cockermouth** (13 miles) near the Cumbrian Coast, with the B5289 making a loop south round Derwentwater via Borrowdale, Buttermere, and Crummock Water and then on to Cockermouth (about 25 miles).

National Express ① *T08705-808080, www.nationalexpress.co.uk*, runs one coach daily leaving London Victoria at 1100 calling at **Kendal** (arrives 1815), **Windermere** (1837), **Ambleside** (1850), **Keswick** (1920) and **Whitehaven** (2015). A standard return to Kendal costs about £35. The quickest journey from London is the overnight coach to Glasgow and Inverness via **Penrith**, leaving London Victoria at 2300 and arriving at 0505. National Express also run three direct coaches to **Carlisle** daily at 1130, 1930 and 2230 (6½ hours).

By train **Oxenholme**, a couple of miles west of Kendal, is the mainline station for the Lakes. Virgin ① *T0870-010 1127, www.virgintrains.co.uk*, runs hourly services from London (three to four hours depending on connections), Carlisle, Preston, Birmingham, the West Country and Manchester. From Oxenholme, a branch line run by **First North Western** ① *www.firstnorthwestern.co.uk*, runs hourly into **Kendal** (five minutes, although it can often be quicker to catch the bus rather than wait for a connection) and on for another 20 minutes calling at **Burneside** and **Staveley** (for summer bus services to Kentmere) to **Windermere**. First North Western also runs the line from Barrow-in-Furness along the Cumbrian coast. For the cheapest tickets see www.thetrainline.com.

Getting around

While a car is undeniably still the most convenient way of getting around the Lakes, the roads are so busy and twisted, especially in summer, that driving can be exhausting. With enough time, easily the best way to explore is on foot or by bicycle, and luckily the local bus network is just about comprehensive enough to make this a practical

The Lake District

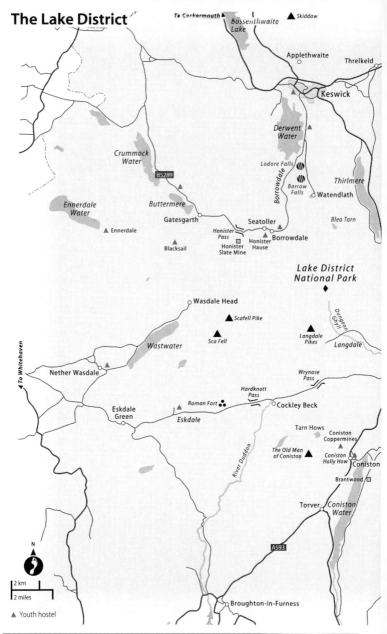

To Cockermouth

Bassenthwaite Lake

▲ Skiddaw

Applethwaite ○

Threlkeld

Keswick

Derwent Water ▲

Crummock Water

B5289

Lodore Falls

Barrow Falls

Borrowdale

Thirlmere

Watendlath ○

Ennerdale Water

Buttermere

Gatesgarth

Blea Tarn

Seatoller ○

Honister Pass

Borrowdale ○

▲ Ennerdale

▲ Blacksail

Honister Slate Mine

Honister Hause

Lake District National Park ♦

Wasdale Head ○

▲ Scafell Pike

Dungeon Ghyll

To Whitehaven ▲

Wastwater

▲ Sca Fell

▲ Langdale Pikes

Langdale

Nether Wasdale ▲

Wrynose Pass

Eskdale Green

Roman Fort ⋰

Hardknott Pass

Cockley Beck ○

Eskdale

Tarn Hows

Coniston Coppermines

River Duddon

The Old Man of Coniston ▲

Coniston Holly How ▲

Coniston

Brantwood ▢

Torver ○

Coniston Water

N

2 km
2 miles

A593

▲ Youth hostel

Broughton-in-Furness ○

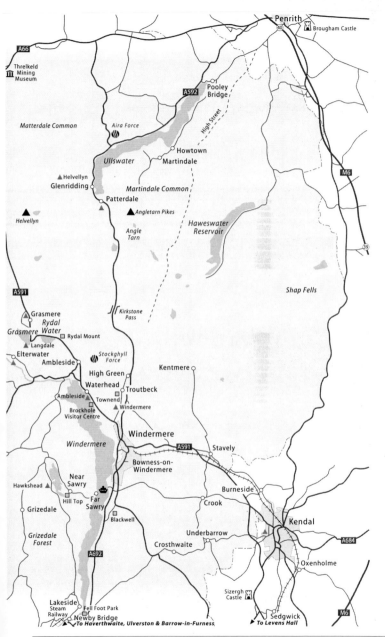

alternative. **Cumbria County Council**, www.cumbria.gov.uk, publishes an indispensable booklet on getting around Cumbria and the Lake District, available from most information centres, complete with timetables, maps and ticket prices. Also useful for planning your journey is **Traveline** ① *T0871-200 2233, www.traveline.info.*

By bicycle Cyclists are in for a treat with miles of country lanes, bridleways and permitted cycleways, as well as a good network of hire points and bike repair workshops. Electric bicycles are becoming popular with 12 hire points and over 30 electric bike charge points. **Windermere Lake Cruises** (see below) runs a Cross-Lakes Shuttlebus service which will transport bikes if you phone in advance. **Stagecoach Cumbria** Route 888 is a special 'bike and ride' service with specially converted buses able to carry up to 12 bikes and riders. The buses travel along the A591 through the heart of the Lakes from Windermere Railway Station to Whinlatter Forest Visitor Centre, stopping at Ambleside, Rydal, Grasmere, Thirlspot, Keswick, and Braithwaite, on the way. The *Coniston Rambler* (see below) also carries bikes free of charge but there's only space for two bikes so book ahead, T01539-4722143. Numerous websites have details of suggested cycle routes including www.golakes.co.uk, www.lakedistrict.gov.uk and www.exploresouthlakeland.co.uk.

By boat Cruising the lake is one of the quintessential Cumbrian experiences and also a useful way to get about, often linking up with other forms of public transport. **Windermere Lake Cruises** ① *T01539-443360, www.windermere-lakecruises.co.uk,* runs regular trips across Lake Windermere to Lakeside, Bowness and Ambleside (see page 25). **Ullswater Steamers** ① *T01768-482229, www.ullswater-steamers.co.uk,* runs heritage cruises the length of the lake from Pooley Bridge to Glenridding (see page 33). Boat trips are also available on Coniston Water with **Coniston Launch** ① *T01768-775753, www.coniston launch.co.uk,* (see page 30) and **Steam Yacht Gondola** ① *T01539-432733, www.national trust.org.uk/gondola,* (see page 30); and on Derwentwater with **Keswick Launch** ① *T01768-772263, www.keswick-launch.co.uk,* (see page 32).

By bus All the main towns are connected by regular bus services, except on Sunday. **Kendal**, **Windermere**, **Ambleside**, **Keswick**, **Hawkshead** and **Coniston** are all connected by at least one bus in any two hours between Monday and Saturday throughout the year. Summer timetables usually operate between 25 March and 26 October. They include: Route 505, the *Coniston Rambler,* from Kendal to Coniston via Windermere, Ambleside and Hawkshead, hourly Monday to Saturday with **Stagecoach in Cumbria**; and Route 555, the *Lakeslink,* from Kendal to Windermere, Ambleside, Grasmere and Keswick, hourly daily with **Stagecoach in Cumbria**. Less frequent routes of particular interest to walkers include Route 541, Monday to Saturday, four buses daily between Kendal, Crook, Underbarrow, Crosthwaite and Windermere; Route 516, the *Langdale Rambler*, six buses daily between Ambleside, Elterwater and Dungeon Ghyll; Route 517, the *Kirkstone Ramber*, three buses on Saturday and Sunday (daily 21 July-31 August) summer only between Bowness, Windermere, Troutbeck, Kirkstone Pass, and Patterdale; and Route 525, the *Mountain Goat*, four buses daily July-September from Hawkshead to Grizedale. Other places that can be reached on summer services only from Keswick include **Watendlath**, **Honister Pass** and **Gatesgarth**.

Stone love

Thrown over most of the northern moors and fells is a slippery net of dry stone walls. They're probably longer in total than the Great Wall of China and even though not visible from space, are one of the most immediately striking features of the north of England. Local variations aside, most are built without mortar, resting on shallow trenches filled with parallel lines of square footing stones, in turn filled with 'heartings' of smaller irregularly shaped rocks. Most were built in the early 19th century, when labour was cheap, and although they require a lot of maintenance today, often the dedicated work of national park volunteers, it's remarkable how many are still standing and in good repair. Coping stones are sometimes placed along the top of the wall to stop sheep jumping over them. Other features of the walls are stoups (posts with holes for bars), hogg holes (for yearling sheep or hogs to pass through), step stiles and squeeze stiles. Even smaller holes at ground level are likely to be rabbit smoots, designed to catch unwary rabbits in a covered pit on the other side.

A variety of special tickets are available. The **North West Explorer** allows unlimited travel on **Stagecoach in Cumbria** buses for one day (£10), three days (£20) or seven days (£25); while the **Cumbria Goldrider** allows unlimited travel on any Stagecoach service for seven days (£23.50) or 28 days (£88). Daily or weekly tickets can be purchased from the driver; other tickets are available from travel shops and tourist information centres.

By train Scenic steam railway routes include the Lakeside and Haverthwaite (see page 26) and Ravenglass and Eskdale (see page 40).

Tourist information
Cumbria has an excellent network of official tourist information centres across the region. The official website of **Cumbria Tourism** is www.golakes.co.uk. There are also some excellent independent tourism centres, which are listed throughout the text. The **Lake District Visitor Centre** ⓘ *Brockdale, between Troutbeck Bridge and Ambleside, T01539-446601, www.lakedistrict.gov.uk, mid-Feb to Nov daily 1000-1700*, is a tourist attraction in itself, with gardens, an adventure playground, putting green and woodland walk, as well as exhibitions, an information desk and café (see page 27).

If you're planning to visit lots of attractions, it might be worth getting a **Freedom of the Lake District Pass**, www.freedomofthelakedistrict.co.uk, which grants admission to numerous attractions in the Lake District at nearly half the cost you'd pay for separate admission to each. The pass can be bought online and printed out. A three-day pass costs £42, a six-day pass costs £65.

If planning on walking in the fells, be aware that the weather can close in quickly. Always check the latest forecast at **Lake District Weatherline** ⓘ *T0870-055 0575, www.lakedistrictweatherline.co.uk*, or tune into *BBC Radio Cumbria* (101FM). Ordnance Survey *Explorer* maps OL4-7 cover the Lake District area.

Kendal and around → *For listings, see pages 42-53.*

Just outside the boundary of the National Park, Kendal is called the 'Gateway to the Lakes' thanks to its proximity to the M6 and the main west coast railway line at Oxenholme. This doughty old market town was built largely out of local limestone and became known as the 'auld grey town'. It's the capital of southeastern Cumbria, most famous for Kendal Mint Cake – a hard-bitten sugar and peppermint sweet favoured by mountaineers – but also closely associated with the 18th-century portrait painter George Romney. (One best-selling brand of Kendal Mint Cake is called Romney's.) Kendal makes a pleasant and relatively inexpensive base from which to explore the Lakes and remains a proper working town, some 7 miles east of all the tourist activity at Windermere and Bowness.

Tourist information
Made in Cumbria ① *25 Stramongate, T01539-735891, www.madeincumbria.co.uk*, is the main point for information. The council website, www.southlakeland.gov.uk, is also useful.

Places in Kendal
Kendal train station is a 10-minute walk from the town centre to the northeast, close to the **Kendal Museum** ① *Station Rd, T01539-815597, www.kendalmuseum.org.uk, Wed-Sat 1030-1700, free.* Only moderately interesting, given its subject matter, this local natural history museum features a stuffed polar bear.

Crossing the River Kent into Stramongate makes for town and passes the **Friends Meeting House** on the left with its modern multicultural Quaker tapestry presenting a chronicle of social history since the 1650s. Stramongate meets the main drag, Highgate, at Finkle Street on the not particularly prepossessing Market Place. It's largely taken up with the **Westmorland Shopping Centre**, www.westmorelandshopping.com, which has recently spawned another, the **Elephant Yard**, www.elephantyard.com, over the street, where you'll find all the usual high street names.

A left turn onto Highgate leads the few yards down to the impressive **Town Hall**, home to some Victorian debating chambers and seriously antique public lavatories. But Kendal's main attraction is the **Abbot Hall Art Gallery** ① *T01539-722464, www.abbothall.org.uk, Mon-Sat 1030-1700, £6.20, combined gallery and museum ticket £8, children free,* by the river near the bottom of Highgate where it becomes Kirkland. One of the country's cutest public art galleries, in an elegant Georgian villa by the river, as well as two almost life-size late-17th-century portraits of the indomitable Lady Anne Clifford, it holds works by local man George Romney, as well as Lakeland scenes by Turner, Ruskin and contemporary art by Lucien Freud and Bridget Riley.

Next door to the Abbot Hall, the **Museum of Lakeland Life and Industry** ① *T01539-722464, www.lakelandmuseum.org.uk, daily 1030-1700, £5, combined museum and art gallery ticket £8, children free,* features recreated traditional Lakeland farmhouse rooms, as well as a reconstruction of Arthur 'Swallows and Amazons' Ransome's study. From here, a riverside walk leads either to **Kendal Parish church** with its Strickland tombs and memorials to local girl Catherine Parr, lucky enough to have been widowed instead of executed by Henry VIII, or over a footbridge up to the hardly spectacular ruins of her birthplace, **Kendal Castle**, but in a fine position overlooking the town and Abbot Hall from the opposite bank of the river.

Back on Highgate, the **Brewery Arts Centre** ⓘ *122A Highgate, T01539-722833, www.breweryarts.co.uk, Mon-Fri0900-2300, Sat 0900-2330, Sun 1000-2230*, is a garden-side arts centre with interesting contemporary art exhibitions and theatre shows, with a good café and reputable restaurant.

Outside Kendal
Sizergh Castle ⓘ *(NT), T01539-560951, estate open daily 0900-1700, house open Mar-Nov Sun-Thu 1300-1700, £10.50, children £5.25*, has been the Strickland family home for over 700 years. A medieval castle redeveloped in the Elizabethan period with an exceptional carved-wood interior, the highlight is the Inlaid Chamber and an outstanding limestone rock garden.

World-famous yew and box topiary, which takes six weeks of clipping each year to maintain, can be seen in the gardens of **Levens Hall** ⓘ *T01539-560321 www.levenshall. co.uk, Apr-Oct Sun-Thu 1200-1630 (house 1200-1600), £12.50, children free.* Laid out in the French style in the late 17th century, the owners of Levens never followed the fashion for Capability Brown landscape and they benefit today. The gardens surround an Elizabethan mansion, home to the Bagot family, that was built around a 13th-century pele tower. Bagot goats with their distinctive horns wander around in the deer park.

Windermere and Bowness-on-Windermere → *For listings, see pages 42-53.*

Windermere, just up the hill on the eastern side of the lake that gave it its name, and neighbouring Bowness, on the shore of the lake itself, are the centre of day tripping Lakeland but hardly typical of the region as a whole. Windermere is quite an attractive jumble of Victorian villas and guesthouses that sprang up after the coming of the railway (fiercely resisted by one William Wordsworth) in the mid-19th century. Bowness-on-Windermere is the Lake District's superbly tacky party prom, a shoreline riddled with cheap and cheerful souvenir shops, heaving with tourists throughout the season and the launch point for cruises on the lake. The landscape visible from this unholy pair is not the most dramatic the Lakes have to offer but very pretty all the same, with low rolling green hills sloping down to a lake often bathed in a cool grey mist.

Getting around
Boat hire is available at Bowness Pier, from where **Windermere Lake Cruises** ⓘ *T01539-443360, www.windermere-lakecruises.co.uk*, runs trips to Waterhead, near Ambleside (single £4.20, return £6.20) at the top of the lake, and Lakeside at the southern end, single £4.30, return £6.40. Combined tickets are available with the **Aquarium of the Lakes** in Lakeside and the Lakeside-Haverthwaite Steam Railway (see below). **Freedom of the Lake** tickets allow unlimited travel on the lake from any pier and cost £11 for 24 hours. A ferry runs across to **Ferry House**, from where it's a long steep climb up to Beatrix Potter's study house at Hill Top in Near Sawrey (see page 31).

Tourist information

Windermere TIC ⓘ *Victoria St, T01539-446499, www.lakelandgateway.info, daily 0900-1700.* **Bowness Bay National Park Information Centre** ⓘ *Glebe Rd, T01539-442895, Apr-Oct daily 1000-1630.*

Places in Windermere and Bowness-on-Windermere

There aren't really many sights in Windermere, although the **Lakeland Plastics** kitchen shop could almost count as one. The main event here remains **Lake Windermere** itself, which is best explored by boat or on one of the local walks. The **Windermere Steamboat Museum** ⓘ *Rayrigg Rd, T01539-445565, www.steamboat.co.uk,* is set to become an impressive feature. Currently being redeveloped and due for completion in 2015, the museum will have a wet dock, exhibition gallery, shop, café overlooking the water conservation workshops and open storage where visitors can view boats waiting to be restored. Check the website for the latest news and special events.

In the meantime, the crowds head down into Bowness-on-Windermere to queue up for the **World of Beatrix Potter** ⓘ *Rayrigg Rd, T01539-488444, www.hop-skip-jump.com, Apr-Sep 1000-1730, Oct-Mar 1000-1630, £6.95, children £3.65,* in the Old Laundry. This see-hear-and-smell show is really only for kids and insatiable fans of Potter, featuring a variety of vaguely threatening much larger-than-life-size characters from the books, including Peter Rabbit and Jemima Puddle-Duck in her 'woodland glade'.

South of Windermere and Bowness

Just over a mile south of Bowness, just off the A5074 on the B5360, **Blackwell** ⓘ *T01539-446139, www.blackwell.org.uk, Mar-Oct daily 1030-1700, Nov-Feb 1030-1600, £7.20, children free,* is an immaculate Arts and Crafts house built for the Manchester brewer Sir Edward Holt in a beautiful position looking towards Coniston Old Man in the last two years of the 19th century. Restored and reopened by the Lakeland Arts Trust in 2001, it now represents one of the finest examples extant of the design movement founded by William Morris in pursuit of locally sourced materials, skills and inspiration. Designed by Mackay Hugh Baillie Scott, it must indeed have made a very welcoming and informal second home away from Victorian Manchester, although the slightly precious atmosphere today hardly evokes the lively family home it might once have been.

Seven miles south of Bowness, **Fell Foot Park** (NT), is a Victorian lakeside pleasure garden restored by the National Trust at the southern end of Lake Windermere. The gardens are at their best in spring or autumn, and there's a tearoom with rowing boat hire in season (April to October).

Round the corner on the opposite side of the lake, beyond Newby Bridge in **Lakeside**, the **Aquarium of the Lakes** ⓘ *T01539-530153, www.lakesaquarium.co.uk, daily 0900-1700, £8.95, children £5.95,* is a good wet-weather attraction, a very comprehensive freshwater aquarium tracing a local river from its source to the sea. Here's the chance to see what ducks get up to while they're underwater, meet an otter or come face to face with a fearsome pike.

The 19th-century **Lakeside and Haverthwaite Steam Railway** ⓘ *T01539-531594, www.lakesiderailway.co.uk, Apr-Oct daily, £5.90 return, children £2.95, combined railway/aquarium and railway/lake cruises tickets available,* forms part of the popular Lakeside complex along with the Aquarium of the Lakes. It was once the iron horse that carried Cumbria's industrial materials, but now it's simply one of the most popular vintage team railways in northern Britain. The 19th-century carriages puff their way up the Leven Valley from Lakeside to Haverthwaite via Newby Bridge and back, with journeys timed to coincide with the arrivals and departures of **Windermere Lake Cruises**.

Ambleside and around → *For listings, see pages 42-53.*

Five miles north of Windermere, beyond the Lake District's main visitor centre at Brockhole and the small village of Troutbeck, Ambleside is the other half of Lakeland's pulsating heart and not very aptly named: this is where the tough get going. None of the ambling lazy pleasures of Bowness and Windermere here. This is a serious hiker town with a fairly forbidding grey-stone look to go with. That said, Ambleside does have a polite and rather sedate side, best appreciated down by the lake where it becomes Waterhead, and has a vaguely bohemian atmosphere in its pubs and cafés. Part of the reason for the town's cachet with hikers is that it's within (serious) walking distance of Windermere station and several strenuous, rewarding climbs can be made right out of the town centre itself.

Tourist information
The **Hub of Ambleside** ① *Central Buildings, Market Cross, T0844-2250544, www.hubof ambleside.co.uk, Mon-Sat 0900-1730, Sun 1000-1700*, is a multi-purpose facility that can help book accommodation, advise on local events and sells essentials such as local guides and fishing permits. Also useful is **Waterhead National Park Information Centre** ① *Waterhead Car Park, near Ambleside, T01539-432729, daily Apr-Oct 1000-1700*, and the website www.amblesideonline.co.uk.

Places in Ambleside
Just out of Windermere on the road to Ambleside, a right turn at Troutbeck Bridge leads the mile up the valley to **Troutbeck**. Just before the village itself, which is the starting point for walks up to viewpoints overlooking Ambleside, the National Trust has preserved a 17th-century yeoman's house at **Townend** ① *(NT), T01539-432628, Mar-Oct Wed-Sun 1300-1700, tours at 1100 and 1300, £4.90, children £2.45*. A remarkable survival, the sturdy whitewashed stone and slate house contains furniture, books and woodwork from the period, very little altered after some 400 years' occupation by the Browne family.

Back on the main A591, halfway between Windermere and Ambleside, the **Lake District Visitor Centre** ① *Brockhole, T01539-446601, www.lakedistrict.gov.uk, daily mid-Feb to Nov daily 1000-1700*, is surrounded by lakeside gardens and contains the latest interactive wizardry to elucidate and entertain visitors about the national park, including a three-dimensional model of the central massif and a gift shop. There's also an adventure playground, putting green and woodland walks.

Just before Waterhead, the **Stagshaw Garden** ① *(NT), T01539-446027, Apr-Oct daily 1000-1830, £1.50*, is a small and little-known woodland garden particularly impressive in the spring, when the azaleas and camellias are in bloom, with walks leading up through the **Skelghyll Woods** to **Jenkins Crag** (half a mile) where there are great views down the length of Lake Windermere.

Ambleside itself is introduced by **Waterhead**, at the head of the lake, with a youth hostel and landing stages for the steamer services and boat hire, about a mile from the centre of the town. A left turn here leads past the attractive lakeside gardens of Borrans Park to the site of the Roman Fort called **Galava**. Little remains of it now except marks in the ground, but its strategic position on the banks of the river Rothay is easy to appreciate.

Since the renovation of the old bus station, the centre of town has moved away from the Market Place into the open area called **Market Cross**, surrounded by shops and cafés that almost manage an Alpine buzz. The rivulet of Stock Ghyll flows into town from the east here, crossed by the Bridge House, apparently built to evade land tax. Further up Rydal Road, the **Armitt Museum** ① *T01539-431212, www.armitt.com, daily 1000-1700 (last admission 1630), £2.50, concessions £1.80, families £5.60*, is the town's interesting local history museum, with finds from Galava Roman Fort and displays on the 19th-century writers and artists that once made Ambleside such a vibrant place: Charlotte Mason, Beatrix Potter, and the Collingwoods. Founded in 1912, the museum is named after Mary Louisa Armitt who gave her library to the town.

The waters of Lake Windermere lap the southern fringe of Ambleside and offer a host of activities including fishing, watersports and lake cruises. ▸▸ *See What to do, page 50.*

Walks
Walks around Ambleside range from the short stroll up to the waterfall of **Stockghyll Force** (less than a mile), to the climb up alongside **The Struggle**, the road that heads up to the **Kirkstone Inn** on Kirkstone Pass (4 miles) over to Ullswater. More serious is the delightful hike over to **High Green** above Troutbeck and up on to the Roman road called **High Street** that runs along the high ridge between Ullswater and Haweswater all the way to Brougham Castle near Penrith (about 15 miles). Details are available from the visitor centre.

West of Ambleside to Wastwater
Beyond the Langdale Valley, the tortuous **Wrynose Pass** climbs up to Cockley Beck at the head of the Duddon Valley before the even steeper **Hardknott Pass** beneath Sca Fell. The road runs by **Hardknott Roman Fort**, an awe-inspiring spot for a legionary outpost overlooking beautiful Eskdale (see page 40). From Eskdale Green a tiny road runs round to **Nether Wasdale** at the foot of **Wastwater**, the deepest, most remote and mysterious of the Lakes, with precipitous scree slopes on its southern side. A difficult road runs along its northern shore all the way to **Wasdale Head**, the most isolated settlement in the entire region. The pub here is suitably serious (many of its customers have walked miles to reach it) and the little church is a moving place too.

Grasmere → *For listings, see pages 42-53.*

Four miles up the road from Ambleside, Grasmere is an undeniably pretty stone-built village five minutes' walk from its own little lake. And it's also the most popular in the Lakes thanks to one William Wordsworth and his younger sister Dorothy, whose homes at Dove Cottage, in the village itself, and at Rydal Mount, on the road up from Ambleside, have been preserved as shrines to the spirit of Lakeland. Although it always becomes very busy with day-trippers in summer, and occasionally dismissive in its attitude to tourists, Grasmere still makes a good base for serious walkers, with wonderful trails west leading up Sour Milk Gill to Easdale Tarn, the Langdale Pikes and over to Borrowdale; or east on to the flanks of Helvellyn, the Lake District's most famous mountain.

Tourist information
There is no tourist office in Grasmere but the website www.grasmere.com offers some useful local information.

Places in Grasmere
First stop from Ambleside on the Wordsworth trail is **Rydal Mount** ① *T01539-433002, www.rydalmount.co.uk, Mar-Oct daily 0930-1700, Nov, Dec, Feb Wed-Sun 1100-1600, closed Jan, £6.75, children £3.25*. The Wordsworths moved into this comfortable whitewashed stone house in 1813 and lived here until 1850. Still owned by their descendants, highlights include the attic room where Wordsworth worked once he was Poet Laureate (although not where he did his best work), the cosy dining room and airy library adding up to an evocative insight into the early Victorian literary life and one of Lakeland's better wet-weather options. The sloping garden was designed and much loved by the great man himself, and his original plantings have been respected. The main road skirts the shoreline of **Rydal Water** on its way into Grasmere. The best views of the small lake are not from this road though but from the fells above, reached on the Grasmere–Eltwater road.

Fans thirsting for more information on the poet, his sister and famous friends will want to press on to **Dove Cottage** ① *T01539-435544, www.wordsworth.org.uk, Mar-Oct daily 0930-1730, Nov-Feb Wed-Mon 0930-1630, £7.80, children £4.50*. They lived here from 1799 to 1808 and the enormously enthusiastic 20-minute guided tours every half hour fill in much of the information missing at Rydal Mount. Coleridge stayed with them here, and the eight-room cottage has been restored to look pretty much as it might have done at the turn of the 19th century. Ticket price includes a modern art gallery and the Wordsworth Museum, packed with memorabilia and trivia related to the influential Lakeland literary circle. Weather-permitting, the garden is included on the tour too. Also in Grasmere, the **Heaton Cooper Studio** ① *T01539-435280, www.heatoncooper.co.uk*, is a permanent celebration of the work of remarkable landscape artist William Heaton Cooper.

A very minor road heads round the little Grasmere lake itself and then climbs steeply up to Elterwater, a charming village on the main hiker's trail up the **Langdale Valley**. Possibly the most popular area with walkers and climbers in the central Lake District, the Langdale Valley can become almost as busy as Grasmere down below.

Hawkshead and Coniston → *For listings, see pages 42-53.*

West of Ambleside, or reached by ferry across Lake Windermere, Hawkshead and Coniston are relatively quieter and less frequented villages. Hawkshead is an attractive place, sitting at the top of tiny Esthwaite Water, below the heights of Near Sawrey (where Beatrix Potter's Hill Top House is the main attraction) and Far Sawrey (for the ferry to Bowness). Coniston is set some way back from Coniston Water itself, a more sedate version of Ambleside, but equally popular with hikers wanting to tackle the Coniston Old Man looming above the village.

Walks in the Lake District

Coniston 11 miles one-way. Start: Coniston village. From Coniston to Langdale along part of the Cumbria Way, through farmland and woods and up to the Dungeon Ghyll Hotel at the feet of Langdale Pikes. OS Maps: *Outdoor Leisure 6.*

Ennerdale 12 miles one-way. Start: Ennerdale Bridge. A hike into the heart of the Lakes through Ennerdale to Seatoller and Borrowdale, past lonely Ennerdale Water and beneath Green Gable. Part of the Coast-to-Coast walk. OS Maps: *Outdoor Leisure 4.*

Harter Fell 8 miles there and back. Start: Kentmere. Quite a stiff climb up alongside the river Kent to a peak of the eastern lakes overlooking Haweswater Reservoir. OS Maps: *Outdoor Leisure 7.*

Great Gable 6 miles there and back. Start: Wasdale Head. A climb up for views down Wastwater from the top of the 2949 ft Great Gable via Sty Head. OS Maps: *Outdoor Leisure 6.*

Blea Tarn 6 miles there and back. Start: Watendlath. A fairly gentle stroll up Borrowdale to the tranquillity of the little Blea Tarn. OS Maps: *Outdoor Leisure 4.*

Getting around

Coniston Launch ① *T01539-436216, www.conistonlaunch.co.uk, Northern cruise £8.50, children £4.25, Southern cruise £11.90, children £5.95,* provides a ferry service to seven jetties, including Brantwood (see below) using 1920s launches powered by solar-electricity. Visitors can use the boat one way and walk back along lakeshore footpaths or access the high fells.

The **Steam Yacht Gondola** ① *(NT), T01539-463850, www.nationaltrust.or.uk/gondola, leaves Coniston Pier Apr-Oct daily at 1100, 1200, 1400, 1500 and 1600, 45-min round-trip £4.80,* is a steam-powered vessel rebuilt from the original Victorian *Gondola*. Visitors can disembark at Brantwood House or Monk Coniston jetty for a circular walk to Tarn Hows.

Tourist information

Hawkshead National Park Information Centre ① *Main Car Park, T01539-436946.*
Coniston National Park Information Centre ① *Main Car Park, Ruskin Av, T01539-441533.*

Places in Hawkshead and Coniston

As Grasmere is to William Wordsworth, so Coniston is to John Ruskin (1819-1900), and it's not too fanciful to think that the differences in the two villages says something about the difference between the two men. Ruskin was inspired by the works of Turner and Wordsworth to find a place of his own in the Lake District. Instead of Rydal Mount, with its cosy situation, he settled at **Brantwood** ① *T01539-441396, www.brantwood.org.uk, Mar-Nov daily 1030-1700, Nov-Mar Wed-Sun 1030-1600, £7.95, children £5.50.* He famously described it as "little more than a hut" when he arrived, but the breathtaking beauty of its position ensured that he persevered until he was inhabiting the fairly grand house it is today. Some way along the eastern shore of the lake, best reached on the splendid steam yacht *Gondola* from Coniston itself, Brantwood is one of the most remarkable houses in the Lake District. Quite apart from the wealth of information on Ruskin's life and work, the place was lived in recently enough for it to remain powerfully redolent of his character. A meticulous genius, many of his ideas are now taken for granted: the dignity of labour, the Welfare State, and the National Trust amongst many others. Visitors can wander the house at will, looking into his drawing room with his piano (well-trained fingers are welcome to try it), his study and his extraordinary dining room with its seven-arched picture window symbolic of the Seven Lamps of Architecture: truth, beauty, memory, life, obedience, power and sacrifice. The gardens also command magnificent views over the lake.

In Coniston itself, the **Ruskin Museum** ① *T01539-441164, www.ruskinmuseum.com, Mar-Nov daily 1000-1730, Nov-Mar Wed-Sun 1030-1530, £5.25, children £2.50,* gives an inspiring insight into the man and his works, including his attempts to improve the local economy and ideas on art and life. Ruskin is buried in the churchyard.

The other man to have left his mark on Coniston was Donald Campbell, who died on the lake attempting to beat his own waterspeed record in 1967. The **Sun Inn**, www.thesunconiston.com, contains a collection of memorabilia associated with his attempts to improve the world waterspeed record first set by his father Malcolm.

Hawkshead is often trumpeted as the 'prettiest village in the Lake District', a claim that could well be justified thanks to the measures that have been taken to keep it that way. Consequently the whole place has an unreal atmosphere: traffic-free, overpriced and often overcrowded. Hawkshead also boasts the **Beatrix Potter Gallery** ① *(NT), Main St, T01539-436355, www.nationaltrust.org.uk/beatrix-potter-gallery, Apr-Oct Mon-Wed, Sat, Sun 1030-1630, £5.30, children £2.40,* in the tiny house that was once her husband's law office, little altered since his day, putting on changing displays of her original artwork for her stories.

In Near Sawrey, **Hill Top** ① *(NT), T01539-436269, mid-Feb to Nov Sat-Thu 1000-1730 with varied seasonal opening hours, £8.50, children £4.25, advance booking advisable,* was the house where Beatrix Potter wrote many of her best-loved stories, and has been kept exactly as she left it, complete with her furniture and china. Mrs Tiggywinkle would feel quite at home here, but she'd have to join the queue like everyone else, unless she'd been a sensible little hedgehog and booked ahead.

South of Hawkshead stretch the 9000 green acres of **Grizedale Forest**, home to the Grizedale sculpture trail, where over 60 contemporary artists have transformed bits of the wood with startling responses to the natural environment since the 1970s. It's also a very popular place for mountain biking. ►► *See What to do, page 50.*

Keswick and around → *For listings, see pages 42-53.*

Keswick is the capital of the Northern Lakes, a lively market town with few pretensions that's very popular with fell walkers. The business end of the Lake District, at the head of lovely Derwentwater on the River Greta, Keswick retains the atmosphere of a hard-working Cumbrian town and makes a good base for exploring Borrowdale, Watendlath and Buttermere. It also has a couple of small museums to kill time if the weather's bad. Scafell Pike, the highest mountain in England, is usually tackled from here or from Langdale. To the north, Skiddaw presents a worthwhile challenge, overlooking peaceful Bassenthwaite Lake.

Getting around

Keswick Launch Company ① *Keswick Lakeshore, T01768-772263, www.keswick-launch. co.uk, year-round 0900-1630 with extended hours in summer; full cruise £9.45, child £4.50; single fares from £2,* runs 50-minute cruises around Derwentwater, with boat landings at seven lakeshore jetties.

Tourist information

Keswick TIC ① *Moot Hall, Market Sq, T01768-772645, www.keswick.org, Apr-Oct daily 0930-1730, Nov-Mar 0930-1630.* Seatoller Barn National Park Information Centre ① *Borrowdale, T01768-777294.*

Places in Keswick

The centre of Keswick is the **Moot Hall**, home to the National Park Information Centre, where the most comprehensive array of leaflets on the Northern Lakes is available. Top of the range of Keswick's attractions is the **Cumberland Pencil Museum** ① *T01768-773626, www.pencilmuseum.co.uk, daily 0930-1700, £4.25, children £3.25, under 5s free,* an unusual and intriguing insight into the history of the humble pencil. The industry in the town as a whole was killed off by technological advances, but one factory remains, manufacturing high-quality graphite Derwent pencils. Somehow inevitably, the museum also boasts the world's largest pencil.

Close competition is provided by **The Puzzling Place** ① *Museum Sq, T01768-775102, www.puzzlingplace.co.uk, Apr-Oct daily 1100-1730, Nov-Mar Tue-Sun 1100-1700, £3.75, children £2.90,* a puzzle museum where gadgets, gizmos, holograms are de rigueur. Check out the anti-gravity room for the best optical illusions.

The **Keswick Museum and Art Gallery** ① *T01768-773263, www.keswickmuseum. org.uk, daily Easter-Oct 1000-1600 but undergoing refurbishment due to reopen Easter 2014, £4.50, children free,* charts the town's mining past with a variety of interesting displays on Lakeland themes, a scale model of the area and the famous 'Musical Stones', an extraordinary sort of stone glockenspiel played by four men.

Around Keswick

Most people come to Keswick to walk, and opportunities abound all around the town. To the north the conifer-clad flanks of Skiddaw beckon, overlooking peaceful Bassenthwaite Lake. Nestling beneath the mountain, **Mirehouse** ① *T01768-772287, www.mirehouse.com, grounds daily 1000-1730, house Wed, Sun (and Fri in Aug) 1400-1700, house and gardens £7.80, children £3.90, gardens only £4, children £2,* is a doughty old lakeside mansion with some fine furniture and a happy family-home atmosphere. Thomas Carlyle and Alfred, Lord Tennyson used to visit here. The piano is played in the living room in summer. The gardens feature a poetry walk and adventure playground and there's a tea room too.

Just west of Keswick, **Whinlatter Forest Park** ① *T01768-778469, www.forestry.gov.uk/ whinlatterforestpark,* boasts some 32 miles of roads and tracks, hence great opportunities for walking, horse riding and orienteering. It's also home to the **Altura Trail**, one of the UK's top mountain biking trails, and the highest **Go Ape** treetop adventure in the country. ▸▸ *See What to do, page 50.*

Three miles east of Keswick off the A66 the **Threlkeld Quarry and Mining Museum** ① *T01768-779747, www.threlkeldquarryandminingmuseum.co.uk, Mar-Oct daily 1000-1700,* *museum £3, children £1.50, mine tour £5, children £2.50*, is one of the best places to get to grips with the Lake District's industrial heritage. As well as a huge variety of different mining implements, large and small, tours of the workings are given by experienced guides, and there's even a chance to pan for gold.

Another more spectacular mine tour is at the **Honister Slate Mine** ① *T01768-777230, www.honister-slate-mine.co.uk, daily 0900-1700, tours 1030, 1230, 1530 (and 1400 in summer), £9.95, children £4.95*, on Honister Pass above Borrowdale, 9 miles from Keswick, where the Westmorland Green Slate has been mined for centuries.

South of Keswick, the B5289 skirts Derwentwater and heads up into **Borrowdale**, many people's favourite Lakeland valley. Sights on the way include the famous **Falls of Lodore**, a waterfall praised to the skies by Robert Southey; the **Barrow Falls**, on the road up to Watendlath, another popular beauty spot, with trails up on to the hills overlooking the mystical little Blea Tarn; and the **Bowder Stone**, an enormous erratic boulder on top of which people climb around. The village of Borrowdale itself is often mobbed with tourists pausing before making the steep ascent up **Honister Pass** beyond Seatoller. After 3 miles the road descends to **Buttermere** and **Crummock Water**, a pair of the most windswept lakes in the district.

Ullswater → *For listings, see pages 42-53.*

The second largest and most northeasterly of the lakes, Ullswater has a special kind of menacing charm that was much appreciated by Wordsworth. Even though roads run down either shore, it often seems unnaturally quiet here. Relatively one of the least congested of the lakes, the road from Pooley Bridge to Glenridding is the most impressive approach by road to Helvellyn (3116 ft), the mountain climber's favourite challenge.

Getting around
Lake cruises are offered by **Ullswater Steamers** ① *Glenridding, T01768-482229, www.ullswater-steamers.co.uk, Freedom of the Lake Pass £12, children £6, (includes half-price voucher for the Ravensglass and Eskdale Railway, see page 40)*. A genteel cruise in three stages (Glenridding Pier House–Howtown Pier–Pooley Bridge Pier House) is a great way to while away a lazy afternoon. The views of England's third-highest mountain, Helvellyn, are amongst the best you will find.

Tourist information
Ullswater National Park Information Centre ① *Main Car Park, Beckside, Glenridding, T01768-482414*. The **Pooley Bridge National Park Information Centre** ① *The Square, T01768-486135*, is operated by **Ullswater Steamers** (see above). The website www.ullswater.co.uk is also useful.

Places in Ullswater
From Pooley Bridge a tiny road runs along the southern shore of the lake to Howtown and then to **Martindale** with its lonely chapel and then on to Dale Head Farm. From Howtown a lovely walk leads up on to **Martindale Common**. **Angle Tarn**, beneath the twin Angletarn Pikes, is one of the most picturesque mountain pools or tarns in the Lake District, with its oddly irregular shape, small islands and popularity with the local herds of red deer.

Three miles before Glenridding, **Aira Force** is an impressive 70-ft waterfall that tumbles down the south face of **Matterdale Common** (where Wordsworth is supposed to have seen his host of nodding daffodils) to the north of the lake. The beck is said to be haunted by the ghost of Sir Eglamore, who made the mistake of waking his somnambulist lover as she wandered around their trysting place mourning his absence. It's a short walk up from the car park on the A5091.

The Lune and Eden valleys → *For listings, see pages 42-53.*

Much less visited than the more dramatic Lake District on the other side of the M6, the valleys of the Lune and the Eden are a lovely pair, embracing one of the most charming forgotten corners of the country. The Lune rises on the Shap Fells in the western Lake District, flowing south through beautiful Borrowdale and down the western flank of the rolling Howgill Fells. It passes below the mountain town of Sedbergh, through doughty little Kirkby Lonsdale and on to the sea at Lancaster. The Eden rises in Mallerstang and flows north past Kirkby Stephen, round the northern edge of the Howgills, through Appleby-in-Westmorland, around Penrith and on to meet the sea beyond Carlisle in the Solway Firth. As well as the wonderful walking country on the fells above, it's the small towns such as Kirkby Lonsdale, Sedbergh, Kirkby Stephen and Appleby-in-Westmorland that make a holiday here so rewarding. Among the most unspoiled in the country, almost untouched by 19th-century heavy industry or 20th-century development, they have so far also managed to resist the worst excesses of 21st-century commercialization. Penrith sits on the northeastern edge of the Lake District on the M6, a convenient and businesslike market town but not much else. To its northwest, reached along a spectacular road, Alston is a high, riverside old town near the meeting of three counties

Arriving in the Lune and Eden valleys

Getting there   The **Leeds–Settle–Carlisle railway**, one of the most scenic in England, is run by **Northern Rail** ① *www.northernrail.org*. Useful stations are Appleby, Kirkby Stephen, and Garsdale (near Sedbergh). Kirkby Stephen station is 1½ miles south of the town itself, on the A685. Garsdale is the closest station to Sedbergh, but the town is most easily reached by bus from Kirkby Stephen, the next stop up the line towards Carlisle, or from Oxenholme mainline station near Kendal. Penrith (about four hours from London Euston via Preston) is the on the same line as Oxenholme, a useful stop for Ullswater and the northeastern Lake District.

Stagecoach ① *www.stagecoachbus.co.uk*, runs three times a day Monday to Saturday from Kendal and Oxenholme mainline station to Sedbergh, Kirkby Stephen, Brough and Darlington. More frequent buses link Brough with Appleby and Penrith (also on the West Coast Main Line).

Tourist information   Kirkby Lonsdale TIC ① *24 Main St, T01524-271437*. **Appleby TIC** ① *Moot Hall, Boroughgate, T01768-351117, www.applebytown.org.uk, Apr-Oct Mon-Sat 0930-1700, Sun 1030-1430, Nov-Mar Mon-Thu 1000-1300, Fri 1000-1500, Sat 1000-1400*. Also try www.appleby.uk.net. **Kirkby Stephen TIC** ① *Market Sq, T01768-371199, www.kirkby-stephen.com, Easter-Oct daily 1000-1700, Nov-Mar Mon-Sat 1000-1700*. **Sedburgh TIC** ① *72 Main St, T01539-620125*. **Penrith TIC** ① *Penrith Museum, T01768-867466, Easter-Oct daily*

Kirkby Lonsdale

Just over the Lancashire border, 5 miles east of Junction 36 on the M6, Kirkby Lonsdale is a delightfully sturdy little 18th-century town clustered round its old market place above the River Lune. Turner sketched the hills around and John Ruskin thought the area one of the loveliest in England. Ruskin's View is a good viewpoint from the churchyard and the church itself has some striking Norman stonework inside and out. A 13-mile walk from the town west to Arnside Moss called **The Limestone Link** is the subject of a well-written leaflet guide available free from the TIC. It passes over the 15th-century **Devil's Bridge**. The A683 up the Lune Valley towards Sedbergh (11 miles) makes for a beautiful drive.

Sedbergh

Sedbergh is another very attractive place, a mountain market town at the meeting point of four valleys and four rivers. Very popular with hikers, it's also the parkland seat of an ancient and hearty public school (past pupils include Will Carling, the former English rugby team captain.) Each year the school stages a gruelling run to the top of **Winder Fell** that looms over the town and provides more superb views. Hidden away up Garsdale in the valley of the River Dee, 5 miles southeast of Sedbergh, is the small village of **Dent**. Once a centre of the local knitting industry – wonderful Herdwick wool sweaters – it's still a popular corner with woolly ramblers, in the far northwest of the Yorkshire Dales National Park, and accessible on the Leeds-Settle-Carlisle railway. The station is a 4-mile walk from the village, in the lea of **Widdale Fell**.

Three miles north of Sedbergh, **Cautley Spout** is a waterfall that drops some 250 yds down a rocky natural amphitheatre beneath the Calf. It's a stiff but rewarding hour-long walk up from the **Cross Keys** temperance hotel. **The Calf** is the 2219-ft peak of the beautiful Howgill Fells. Much softer in look and on the legs than the Lake District, these fells were the favourite of A. Wainwright, whose meticulously handwritten, illustrated and mapped walking guides reintroduced the joys of hillwalking to a generation in the late 1960s and early 1970s.

Kirkby Stephen

The lovely A683 continues for another 14 miles up to Kirkby Stephen, an important staging post on Wainwright's popular **Coast-to-Coast** walk and voted 'England's Best Village' in 2009. Strung out along the main road, this solid-looking town is still very much the working centre of its region, yet to have its character completely altered by the demands of tourism. On the main Market Square a Georgian loggia stands in front of the impressive church, which contains a mysterious eighth-century Anglo-Danish relic called the **Loki Stone**. The only one of its type in England, it's a remarkable survival, apparently the earliest known depiction of the devil in human form – the troublemaking Norse god Loki in horns and chains.

The source of the river Eden lies some 10 miles south up the Mallerstang Valley via Outhgill on the B6259. The river is already a significant obstacle as it flows past the east side of the town. Three miles down this mysterious and lonely valley road are the ruins of little

Pendragon Castle. On a small mound beside the river, this was supposedly where King's Arthur's father Uther was poisoned. Like the castles at Brough, Appleby and Brougham, it was restored in the 17th century by the indefatigable wandering medievalist Lady Anne Clifford. Since then it has become a very quiet and picturesque ruin.

Appleby-in-Westmorland

Tucked into a loop in the river 12 miles northwest of Kirkby, Appleby-in-Westmorland is a delightful, old red-stone riverside town, solid and castellated. Once the county town of Westmorland, it's a sort of mini-Edinburgh with its **castle** at the top of its cobbled main street, Boroughgate, columns at either end marking the extent of the market and battered old church behind a colonnade at the bottom. The church, like the castle, was restored by Lady Anne Clifford, and contains one of the oldest organ cases in the country, as well as the memorial chapel to the great woman herself. The draped effigy of her mother was apparently carved by the same hand as that of Elizabeth I in Westminster Abbey.

Penrith

Sitting next to junction 40 on the M6, Penrith is a fairly unprepossessing market town on the main west coast railway line that makes a useful launch pad for Ullswater and the northeastern Lakes. There's not a huge amount to see in the town, apart from the small **Penrith Museum** ⓘ *Robinson's School, Middlegate, T01768-865105, www.eden.gov.uk/ museum, Mon-Sat 1000-1700, Apr-Oct Sun 1300-1645, free*, and the ruined castle, but its specialist shops make for some rewarding browsing. Southeast of town, however, **Brougham Castle** ⓘ *(EH), T01768-862488, Apr-Sep daily 1000-1800, Oct-Mar Sat-Sun 1000-1600, £3.90, children £2.30,* is beautifully situated on the banks of the River Eamont. The castle was involved in border disputes throughout its early history, and the ruin was taken in hand by Lady Anne Clifford in the late 17th century. Today it remains one of the most impressive examples of her restorations.

A few miles south of Penrith, **Lowther Castle and Garden** ⓘ *T01931-712192, www.lowthercastle.org, gardens £8, children free*, was built in 1806 on a site occupied by the Lowther family for 800 years. The castle was requisitioned by the army during the Second World War and returned to the family in poor condition. Since then it has undergone extensive restoration and is now open to the public.

Six miles northwest of Penrith, **Hutton-in-the-Forest** ⓘ *T01768-484449, www.hutton-in-the-forest.co.uk, house and gardens £9, children £3, gardens only £6, children free, house May-Sep Wed, Thu, Sun 1230-1600, gardens Apr-Oct Sun-Fri 1100-1700,* is a historic Cumbrian house built over six periods between 14th and 19th centuries reflecting the country house style of the time. The gardens date back to the 17th century and host a variety of outdoor events in summer including outdoor theatre, horse trials and Potfest in the Park.

Alston

Northwest of Penrith, the A686 heads up on to the North Pennines via the village of **Melmerby** (famous for its organic bakery) affording spectacular views over the Lakeland hills and Eden Valley before it reaches **Alston**, the highest market town in England. It's a stone-built, old-fashioned place in the middle of nowhere on the South Tyne River and the Pennine Way, close to the meeting of Cumbria, Northumberland and County Durham.

The Cumbrian coast: Grange-over-Sands to Cockermouth

Between the Lakeland mountains and the Irish Sea, the Cumbrian Coast is a strange, embattled, but in places very beautiful region, largely overlooked by many Lakeland tourists. Most immediately attractive and accessible are its southern fringes, known as the Furness Peninsulas. This broken, heavily indented coastline spreads out into the sandflats of Morecambe Bay around the shipbuilding and gas-terminal port of Barrow-in-Furness, defined by the silted estuaries of the rivers Kent, Leven and Duddon. Grange-over-Sands is the main town on the smaller eastern peninsula, the traditional landing point of the route over the sands once used by the monks and nuns of Cartmel Priory.

The village of Cartmel is still the main attraction, along with the famous gardens at Holker Hall. The larger promontory to the west boasts the lively market town of Ulverston before petering out with the industrial sprawl of Barrow at its tip. The port does draw in a few visitors with its interesting dockside museum, some superb nature reserves and small boat trips out to Piel Island and its ruined castle. Broughton-in-Furness is a dignified little town that sits at the root of the peninsula near the mouth of the Duddon. The coast road and railway then sneak round the bulk of Black Combe, with its extraordinary panoramic views, and head north, past pretty Ravenglass, where Eskdale meets the sea. Beyond St Bees Head, the dramatic starting point for Wainwright's Coast-to-Coast walk, Whitehaven introduces the abandoned industrial wasteland and marshes of the northern stretches of the coast. Inland, Cockermouth is a gritty but fine Georgian-looking town on the edge of the northwestern Lakes.

Arriving at the Cumbrian coast

Getting there A car is easily the most convenient way of exploring the coast, although the train and bus service is significantly more reliable and regular than elsewhere in Cumbria. From Junction 36 on the M6 the A590 leads to Ulverston and Barrow-in-Furness. Off this big road, the A595 is reached via the A5092 and runs all the way round the coast back to Carlisle at the top of the M6. **National Express** ① *T08705-808080, www.nationalexpress.co.uk*, runs coaches to Kendal from where the X35 runs to Ulverston and Barrow-in-Furness. Cartmel can be reached by bus from Grange-over-Sands.

The **Furness Line** ① *www.furnessline.co.uk*, from Lancaster to Carlisle also runs right round the coast, calling at Grange-over-Sands, Ulverston, Barrow-in-Furness, Ravenglass, Seascale, St Bees, Whitehaven, and Maryport, among other places. See also the websites www.cumbriancoastline.co.uk and www.lakesline.co.uk.

Tourist information Grange-over-Sands TIC ① *Victoria Hall, Main St, T01539-534026.* **Barrow-in-Furness TIC** ① *Forum 28, Duke St, T01229-876505, www.barrowtourism.co.uk.* **Ulverston TIC** ① *Coronation Hall, T01229-587120. Mon-Sat 0900-1700.* **Cockermouth TIC** ① *Kings Arms Lane, T01900-822634.* The websites www.cockermouth.org.uk, www.white haven.org.uk, www.western-lakedistrict.co.uk and www.lakelandgateway.info are also a good source of information.

Grange-over-Sands

Grange-over-Sands is a solid-looking Victorian seaside town with a breezy prom overlooking Morecambe Bay. Otherwise there's not much to keep visitors here long.

Some will no doubt want to head off on foot on the 33-mile **Cistercian Way** to Piel Island via Cartmel and Ulverston that starts here. Its first leg heads up through the yew tree woods of Eggerslack onto Hampsfell, with wide-reaching views of the muddy bay. Grange was also once the landing point of the short-cut over the sands from Lancaster to the Lake District taken by the monks of Cartmel and Furness Abbeys.

Cartmel, a couple of miles west, just inland, is the most popular and also one of the most attractive little villages in these parts, clustered around the remains of its 12th-century **priory** ① *(NT), Cartmel Priory Gatehouse, Cavendish St, T01539-536874, www.cartmelpriory.org.uk, Easter-Oct Wed-Sun 1000-1600, Nov-Mar Sat, Sun 1000-1600.* The church survived the Dissolution, thanks to also being the place of worship for the parish, and is still a very fine building indeed. Restored by the Preston family of Holker Hall in the 17th century, its bell tower sits at an angle to the main church. Inside, highlights include the stained glass, medieval chancel, Jacobean screen and carved choir stalls. The gatehouse of the priory is also still standing, thanks to being a grammar school in the 17th and 18th centuries, and is now in the care of the National Trust, containing displays on the history of the village, priory and the peninsula.

Five miles west of Grange on the B5277, the main part of **Holker Hall** ① *Cark-in-Cartmel, T01539-558328, www.holker.co.uk, Mar-Nov Sun-Fri 1100-1600, £11.50, children free*, was built in the 1870s for William Cavendish, the Seventh Duke of Devonshire, and represents Victorian country house style at its best. Still the home of Lord and Lady Cavendish, the interior of the house is warm and welcoming, decorated with an impressive variety of antiques and Old Masters, but it's the gardens that have made the house famous. Vaguely Italianate in style, they feature a limestone cascade, sunken garden and a fountain. The **Garden Festival** held in the first week of June is one of the most prestigious in the country.

Previously in the grounds of Holker Hall, the **Lakeland Motor Museum** ① *Old Blue Mill, Backbarrow, T01539-530400, www.lakelandmotormuseum.co.uk, £7.80, children £5*, moved to new expanded premises at Backbarrow, 7 miles north. The collection comprises over 30,000 exhibits and traces the history of motor transport through to the present day with some fascinating memorabilia including veteran vehicles share and an exhibition devoted to Donald Campbell, the waterspeed record-breaker.

Ulverston

From Holker Hall, the shifting sands of the Leven estuary can be crossed on foot with the guidance of Mr Raymond Porter, T01229-580935. It's a wonderful and bracing way to reach Ulverston or Conishead Priory on the opposite bank. Ulverston is a delightful old market town, complete with cobbled streets, ancient alleys and a vigorous local life. The most famous performer associated with the town remains Arthur Jefferson, aka Stan Laurel. He was born here and went on to find success in Hollywood, a career lovingly charted for fans at the exhaustive **Laurel and Hardy Museum** ① *On Stage at the Roxy, Brogden St, T01229-582292, www.laurel-and-hardy.co.uk, daily except Mon and Wed 1000-1700, £4.50, children £2.50*. The town is overlooked from the north by the monument to the founder of the Royal Geographical Society, Sir John Barrow, on Hoad Hill, which commands fine views. The other great man associated with Ulverston is George Fox, who founded Quakerism at Swarthmoor Hall to the south of the town. The **Cumbria Way** is a long-distance footpath that runs from here to Carlisle for 70 miles.

Two miles south of the town, **Conishead Priory** ⓘ *Priory Rd, near Ulverston, T01229-584029, www.conisheadpriory.org, Mar-Oct Mon-Sat 1100-1700, Sun 1200-1700, winter daily 1200-1600, £3.50, children free*, was designed by the son of James Wyatt for Thomas Bradyll in the early 19th century on the site of a 12th-century convent. Its architecture is an extraordinary combination of neo-Elizabethan and neo-Gothic and it has been restored by the Buddhist **Manjushri Kadampa Meditation Centre**, www.manjushri.org, who have built a temple housing an 8-ft Buddha in the gardens. They offer accommodation, courses and retreats as well as light refreshments.

Barrow-in-Furness

At the end of the peninsula, Barrow-in-Furness was developed in the mid-19th century by William Cavendish of Holker Hall as a port for iron ore and then steel. It became one of the main shipbuilding yards in the country and now relies on the handling of nuclear fuel and gas for most of its income. The town's main attraction is the **Dock Museum** ⓘ *North Rd, T01229-876400, www.dockmuseum.org.uk, Wed-Sun 1100-1600, free*, with models of the ships that have been constructed here, and interesting displays on the development of the town.

Just before Barrow-in-Furness, **Furness Abbey** ⓘ *(EH), Manor Rd, T01229-823420, www.furnessabbey.org.uk, Apr-Oct daily 1000-1800, Oct daily 1000-1700, Nov-Mar Sat-Sun 1000-1600, £3.90, children £2.30*, was founded in the early 12th century by Savigniac monks and enlarged shortly afterwards by the Cistercians. Once one of the most important monasteries in the north of England, its situation today hardly bears comparison with its more famous cousins in Yorkshire, but enough has survived to give a good impression of the life led by the monks before the Dissolution. The other main draw from Barrow is the 14th-century **Piel Castle** ⓘ *(EH), T01229-835809*, now in ruins, built to defend Furness Abbey from the Scots. It sits lonely and remote on Piel Island, reachable by an erratic small-boat ferry from Roa Island. On the island, which was given to the people of Barrow by the Duke of Buccleuch in memory of their dead in the First World War, the *Ship Inn* provides hearty refreshments.

Off the A590 to Barrow, clearly signposted, the **South Lakes Wild Animal Park** ⓘ *Broughton Rd, T01229-466086, www.wildanimalpark.co.uk, daily 1000-1630, tiger feeding daily 1430-1500, £13.50, children £8, Nov-Feb free*, claims to be Europe's top tiger sanctuary. Thanks to some cunning landscape design, animals as diverse as kangaroos, monkeys, rhinos, lions, apes and giraffes appear to be wandering free over about 17 acres. Recent arrivals, the only ones in England, are the spectacled bears. The tiger feeding each afternoon is very popular.

Around Black Combe

Just within the National Park, at the top of the peninsula, **Broughton-in-Furness** is an old stone-built town with an attractive market square where the fish slabs, stocks and obelisk celebrating the coronation of George III still survive. From here the A593 runs up into the Lake District and Coniston Water, a small road branching off left up the relatively unexplored valley of the river Lickie with lovely walks above Broughton Mills.

Just before Duddon Bridge, on the main A595 coast road, another small road leads north up the Duddon Valley to **Ulpha**. A favourite of Wordsworth's, the rolling fells embracing the Duddon Valley remain surprisingly undiscovered compared to much of the Lake District. The coast road continues through Whicham, from where an easy path leads up to the **Black Combe**, rising to 1970 ft and providing one of the most spectacular views in the country from its heathery summit. On a clear day the panorama includes the Isle of Man and Ireland beyond to the west, as well as the main peaks of the Lake District to the east.

Eskdale

Ten miles further up the coast, **Ravenglass** is a little village sitting at the bottom of Eskdale and is the start of the **Ravenglass and Eskdale Steam Railway** ① *T01229-717171, www.ravenglass-railway.co.uk, Mar-Nov daily, Dec-Feb weekends only, see website for running times, £12.80, children £6.40, bicycles £3 book in advance*. One of Wainright's favourite journeys, the miniature railway winds its way through 7 miles of spectacular scenery to Dalegarth-for-Boot. Originally built to carry iron ore, and known as **La'al Ratty**, it's a big hit with grown-ups and kids.

From Ravenglass the road climbs up the valley of the Esk and into the Lakes via Hardknott and Wrynose passes, the only road eastwards and hence often jammed. (The only other way back into the Lakes is all the way round to the north via Cockermouth and Keswick).

More family fun is on offer at **Muncaster Castle** ① *T01229-717614, www.muncaster. co.uk, Mar-Oct Gardens and Owl Centre daily 1030-1800 (or dusk if earlier), castle Mon-Fri, Sun 1030-1800 (or dusk if earlier) £13, children £7.50*, home of the **World Owl Centre**, the largest collection of the wise birds in the world, and there's also the opportunity of taking an interactive wand tour of the castle's interior, still home to the Pennington family after 800 years.

Along this stretch of coast is the **Sellafield Centre**, www.sellafieldsites.com. There are no longer regular tours of this nuclear reprocessing facility for security reasons but a small section is still open to the public at selected times. Calder Hall, nearby, was the first nuclear power station to be commissioned in Britain, and Sellafield was originally designed to cope with its spent rods. It is in the process of being decommissioned.

St Bees Head and Whitehaven

Somehow Sellafield and its heavy industrial buildings set the bleak and sadly unprepossessing tone for the rest of the Cumbrian Coast to the north. The relatively dramatic cliffs of St Bees Head are a glorious exception, popular with puffins and seals, and there's an excellent little overhanging cave system at **Fleswick Beach**. This is close to the start of Wainwright's Coast-to-Coast walk to Robin Hood's Bay on the North Yorkshire coast. **Cleator**, 5 miles west of the headland was the birthplace of **Kangol**, one of the most fashionable names in headgear; the factory outlet store has now closed.

Round the corner from St Bees, the relatively large town of Whitehaven, developed on a grid plan by the Lowther family, was heavily involved in the 18th-century sugar, rum and slave trade. Their Georgian church of St James's survives at the top of the town on Queen Street, but much of the rest of the town has suffered badly since. It has recently had a facelift on its harbourfront though, including attractions such as **The Beacon** ① *West Strand, T01946-592302, www.thebeacon-whitehaven.co.uk, Wed-Sat 1100-1600, Sun 1200-1600, £5.50, children £1*, the town's local history museum, including a Met Office gallery, the story of the town's mining heritage, and the founder of the US navy, privateer John Paul Jones's attempted attack on the town, as well as the *Whitehaven Quest*, an information pack detailing 10 historical trails round the area. **The Rum Story** ① *Lowther St, T01946-592933, www.rumstory.co.uk, daily 1000-1700, £5.50, children £3.45*, in the new Historic Harbour development, tells some of the story of the town's slaving history, with dummies in dioramas, spiced up with stories of the rum trade thanks to its location in Jefferson's late-18th-century shop and bonded warehouses.

Cockermouth
Thirteen miles northeast of Whitehaven and 7 miles inland, Cockermouth is a hard-bitten but good-looking farming town. Its main visitor attraction is the National Trust's **Wordsworth House and Garden** ① *(NT), Main St, T01900-824805, www.wordsworth house.org.uk, £7, children £3.50*, where Dorothy and William were born. Their large house has been filled with a few mementoes, but it's not the most engaging of stops on the Wordsworth trail. Monthly changing exhibitions by local artists can be seen at the impressive Georgian home of the **Castlegate House Gallery** ① *T01900-822149, www.castlegatehouse.co.uk, daily 1000-1700 (Tue and Sun by appointment), free.*

Maryport
Maryport, the last town of much importance on the coast, with a dinky little harbour, can boast the **Lake District Coast Aquarium** ① *South Quay, T01900-817760, www.coast aquarium.co.uk, daily 1000-1700, £7.50, children £4.75*, and the **Senhouse Roman Museum** ① *The Battery, Sea Brows, T01900-816168, www.senhousemuseum.co.uk, Nov-Mar Fri-Sun 1030-1600, Apr-Jun daily except Mon and Wed 1000-1700, Jul-Oct daily 1000-1700, £3, children £1*, with its altar stones, household gods, mysterious Serpent Stone and observation tower, next to the site of Alauna Roman fort at the end of Hadrian's Wall.

Cumbria and the Lake District listings

For hotel and restaurant price codes, and other relevant information, see pages 9-12.

● Where to stay

The Lake District is packed with self-catering options, from mansions to bothies. Endless different campsites are on offer; details from the local tourist office. Free range camping is not exactly encouraged, but if done carefully on National Trust land (most of the central range) without disturbing the environment in any way at all, no one's likely to mind. The other option is one of the 25 youth hostels. They usually need to be booked well in advance and many are not open in winter, so it's best to ring first. Facilities also vary quite widely. More basic still, but in the most glorious positions, are the range of YHA camping barns. There are at least 10 dotted around the Lake District, many within walking distance of each other, but they too need to booked ahead some time in advance especially in high season. Not all are open all year. Contact **Lakeland Barns Booking Office**, T01768-774301, www.lakelandcampingbarns.co.uk.

Camping barns (No of beds): **Blake Beck** (12), **Catbells** (12), **Cragg** (8), **Dinah Hoggus** (12), **Fell End** (12), **High Gillerthwaite** (14), **Hudscales** (12), **St John's-in-the-Vale** (8), **Swallow** (18), **Swirral** (8). Cost £4 per person per night.

Kendal and around *p24*
There are numerous other B&Bs in Kendal; details from the tourist information centres.
££ Ardrig Vegetarian B&B, 144 Windermere Rd, T01539-736879, www.ardrigvegetarian.com. Quiet, friendly B&B providing simple accommodation and vegetarian/organic food.
££ Bridge House B&B, 65 Castle St, T01539-722041, www.bridgehouse-kendal.co.uk. Small B&B in a beautiful Georgian building and former station-master's house. Drying facilities, Wi-Fi.
££ The Glen, Oxenholme, T01539-726386, www.glen-kendal.co.uk. A small friendly guesthouse on outskirts of town. Above Oxenholme station, close to the pub.
££ Hillside B&B, 4 Beast Banks, T01539-722836, www.hillside-kendal.co.uk. Central B&B with 6 en suite rooms, parking for guests.
£ Kendal Hostel, 118 Highgate, T01539-724066. With 54 beds in the middle of town close to the Brewery Arts Centre.

Outside Kendal *p25*
££££-£££ The Punch Bowl, Crosthwaite Lyth Valley, T01539-568237, www.the-punchbowl.co.uk. 9 luxury en suite rooms with under-floor heating, free-standing baths and flatscreen TV. Full Cumbrian breakfast included. Restaurant and bar downstairs.

Self-catering
£££-££ Burrow Hall Country Guest House, Plantation Bridge, Staveley, T01539-821711, www.burrowhall.co.uk. 2 miles outside Kendal, an old Lakeland house with 2 self-catering cottages tastefully furnished, in peaceful countryside.

Windermere and Bowness *p25*
££££ Gilpin Lodge, Crook Rd, Windermere, T01539-488818, www.gilpin-lodge.co.uk. There's a small country house atmosphere but with luxury accommodation, top-notch food and a spa. A real treat.
£££ Miller Howe, Rayrigg Rd, Windermere, T01539-442536, www.millerhowe.com. A longstanding 'luxury hotel' with a reputation for its excellent food. Great views over the fells and lake.
£££ Storrs Gate House, Bowness-on-Windermere, T01539-443272, www.storrsgatehouse.co.uk. Country house B&B in a secluded location. Full of old-world charm.

£££-££ The Cottage Guest House, Elleray Rd, Windermere, T01539-444796, www.thecottageguesthouse.com. A family-run guesthouse, most rooms have en suite bathrooms. Close to the station.

£££-££ Jerichos Guest House, College Rd, T01539-442522, www.jerichos.co.uk. Central family-run guesthouse with original Victorian period features refurbished to a high standard. Wi-Fi, parking, breakfast.

££ The Coppice Guest House, Brook Rd, Windermere, T01539-488501, www.thecoppice.co.uk. Guesthouse with quality food, all home prepared. Well-behaved pets welcome.

££ Lowfell B&B, Ferney Green, Bowness-on-Windermere, T01539-445612, www.low-fell.co.uk. Lakeland stone country house a few mins' walk from the lake and village. Secluded gardens, comfortable beds.

££-£ Green Gables Guest House, 37 Broad St, Windermere, T01539-443886, www.greengablesguesthouse.co.uk. A good-value family-run guesthouse in the town with lounge bar, most rooms have en suite bathrooms.

£ Windermere YHA, Bridge Lane, Troutbeck, T01539-443543. With 69 beds in a panoramic position above the town, good for gentle walks through the woods.

Ambleside and around p27

£££ Drunken Duck Inn, Barngates, T01539-436347, www.drunkenduckinn.co.uk. Lakeside retreat set within 60 acres of private land. Price includes breakfast, afternoon tea and use of leisure facilities.

£££ Nanny Brow, Clappersgate, T01539-433232, www.nannybrow.co.uk. Just west of Ambleside, Arts & Crafts house surrounded by ancient woodland. Excellent views, very comfortable.

£££ The Waterwheel Guesthouse, 3 Bridge St, T01539-433286, www.waterwheel ambleside.co.uk. Charming cottage in the heart of the village.

£££-££ Elder Grove Hotel, Lake Rd, Ambleside, T01539-432504, www.elder grove.co.uk. Victorian house with 10 rooms and private car park.

£££-££ Riverside, Under Loughrigg, at the other end of Ambleside, T01539-432395, www.riverside-at-ambleside.co.uk. 5-room family-run B&B overlooking river. 10 mins from the centre.

£££-££ Wasdale Head Inn, Wasdale Head, T01946-726229, www.wasdale.com. Venerable walkers' and climbers' pub with a serious atmosphere and comfortable rooms. At the same site, **Lingmell House** is a charming B&B with cheaper rooms.

££ Claremont House, Compston Rd, Ambleside, T01539-433448, www.claremont ambleside.co.uk. Family-run, friendly, 8 rooms most with en suite bathrooms.

££ Meadowbank Guesthouse, Rydal Rd, Ambleside, T01539-432710, www.meadowbank.org.uk. Set in its own grounds with views of fells.

££ Walmar Hotel, Lake Rd, Ambleside, T01539-432454, www.walmar-ambleside. co.uk. Victorian house with off-street parking, family-run, 8 rooms with en suite bathrooms.

£ Ambleside YHA, Waterhead, Ambleside, T01539-432304. With 245 beds in 43 2-5-bedded rooms and 16 6-8 bedded rooms, near the landing stages for the lakes.

£ Elterwater YHA, Elterwater, near Ambleside, T01539-437245. With 45 beds in the last village in Langdale, very popular with climbers.

£ Langdale YHA, High Close, Loughrigg, near Ambleside, T01539-432304. With 96 beds in a Victorian mansion owned by the National Trust.

£ Wastwater YHA, Wasdale Hall, Wasdale, T01946-726222 with 50 beds in an imposing National Trust property on the edge of Wastwater. One of the most dramatically situated youth hostels in the Lakes.

Camping

Great Langdale National Trust Campsite, Great Langdale, Ambleside, T01539-437668, www.langdalecampsite.org.uk. Beautiful location and good facilities.

Low Wray National Trust Campsite, Low Wray, near Ambleside, T01539-432810, www.lowwraycampsite.org.uk. Lakeside camping but gets busy, book ahead.

Wasdale Head Campsite, Seascale, T01946-726220, www.ntlakescampsites.org.uk. Good wilderness location for hiking.

Grasmere p28

£££ Bridge House Hotel, Church Bridge, Grasmere, T01539-435425, www.bridgehousegrasmere.co.uk. Family-owned hotel beside the River Rothay with peaceful woodland gardens.

£££ The Grasmere Hotel, Broadgate, Grasmere, T01539-435277, www.grasmerehotel.co.uk. Quiet location with 13 rooms, Victorian house renowned for the quality of its food.

£££ Heidi's Grasmere Lodge, Red Lion Sq, Grasmere, T01539-435248, www.heidisgrasmerelodge.co.uk. Small, traditionally built, family-run quiet guesthouse in the centre of the village with 6 rooms.

£££ Moss Grove Organic Hotel, Grasmere T01539-435211, www.mossgrove.co.uk. Some 4-poster beds with balconies, conservatory, sauna, free use of nearby indoor pool in the Wordsworth.

£££ Oak Bank Hotel, Broadgate, Grasmere, T01539-435217, www.lakedistricthotel.co.uk. Nestled in Grasmere village, with 2 comfortable guest lounges, Wi-Fi and good cooking. River at the bottom of the garden.

££ Dunmail House, Keswick Rd, Grasmere, T01539-435256, www.dunmailhouse.com. Small, friendly family-run guesthouse with 3 doubles.

££ Gold Rill Hotel, Red Bank Rd, Grasmere, T01539-435486, www.gold-rill.com. Awards for hospitality and its restaurant at this hotel with 25 rooms, 8 with lake views. A couple of mins' walk from the village.

££ How Foot Lodge, Townend, Grasmere, T01539-435366, www.howfootlodge.co.uk. Victorian country guest house, close to lake, 6 spacious bedrooms with nice views.

££ Old Dungeon Ghyll Hotel, Great Langdale, T01534-937272, www.odg.co.uk. Basic but practical enough, the classic Lakeland mountaineer's pub, with 14 bedrooms and the hiker's bar in a magnificent position beneath the Langdale Pikes.

£ Grasmere Butharlyp How YHA, Easedale Rd, Grasmere, T01539-435316. With 82 beds close to the heart of the village and very popular with walkers.

£ Grasmere Thorney How Hostel, Easdale Rd, Grasmere T01539-435597, www.thorneyhow.co.uk. Independent hostel with 53 beds, smaller and more secluded than the other Grasmere hostel, also a favourite with ramblers.

Hawkshead and Coniston p29

£££ Bank Ground Farm, east of the lake, T015394 41264, www.bankground.com. Grade II listed 15th-century farmhouse on the lake with B&B or self-catering options.

£££-££ Waterhead Hotel, Coniston, T01539-441244, www.waterhead-hotel.co.uk. A 21-room hotel lying in its own grounds with private jetty and rowing boats.

££ Sun Inn Hotel, Coniston, T01539-441248, www.thesunconiston.com. Family-run hotel with views of the fells, good food and ales, 10 rooms with en suite bathrooms.

£ Coniston Coppermines YHA, Coniston, T01539-441261 with 28 beds in a beautiful mountain setting above Coniston village, ideal for taking on the Coniston Old Man.

£ Coniston Holly How YHA, Far End, Coniston T01539-441323. With 60 beds and within walking distance of the village.

£ **Hawkshead YHA**, Hawkshead, T01539-436293. With 109 beds in a Regency mansion overlooking Esthwaite Water, popular with families.

Self-catering
Yew Tree Farm, Coniston, T015394 41433, http://yewtree-farm.com. Self-catering accommodation on a working farm once owned by Beatrix Potter which featured in the film *Miss Potter*. Beautiful location.

Keswick and around *p31*
££££-£££ **Cottage in the Wood**, Magic Hill, Whinlatter Forest, T01768-778409, www.thecottageinthewood.co.uk. Former 17th-century coaching inn, tranquil setting with great views, luxurious accommodation.
£££ **Borrowdale Gates Hotel**, Grange-in-Borrowdale, T01768-777204, www.borrowdale-gates.com. Country house with log fires, home-cooked food and warm comfortable rooms.
£££ **Lyzzick Hall**, Under Skiddaw, T01768-772277, www.lyzzickhall.co.uk. Superb views and a beautiful garden at this old manor house hotel with a swimming pool.
£££ **Swinside Lodge Hotel**, Newlands Valley, T01768-772948, www.swinsidelodge-hotel.co.uk. Intimate country house with stunning views, close to Derwentwater, elegant rooms, excellent food.
£££-££ **Hazeldene Hotel**, The Heads, Keswick, T01768-772106, www.hazeldene-hotel.co.uk. Views over the fells on the outskirts of town, family-run, and good food.
££ **Acorn House Hotel**, Ambleside Rd, Keswick, T01768-772553, www.acornhouse hotel.co.uk. A comfortable Georgian house near the town centre with colourful gardens.
££ **Greystones Hotel**, Ambleside Rd, Keswick, T01768-773108, www.greystones keswick.co.uk. Small, well-appointed guesthouse within walking distance of both town centre and lake.

£ **Borrowdale YHA**, Longthwaite, Borrowdale, T01768-777257. With 88 beds in 2- to 8-bed rooms, a cedarwood cabin beside the river.
£ **Buttermere YHA**, Buttermere, T01768-770245. With 70 beds in an old farmhouse at the foot of Honister Pass.
£ **Derwentwater Hostel**, Barrow House, Borrowdale, near Keswick, T01768-777246. Independent hostel with 88 beds, in an 18th-century mansion overlooking the lake.
£ **Ennerdale YHA**, Cat Crag, Ennerdale, T01946-861237. With 24 beds, basic facilities at the head of the lake.
£ **Honister Hause YHA**, Seatoller, near Keswick, T01768-777267. With 26 beds, high up on Honister Pass, within strenuous walking distance of the highest summits in the Lakes.
£ **Keswick YHA**, Station Rd, Keswick, T01768-772484. With 91 beds close to the river and the centre of town.
£ **Skiddaw House YHA**, Bassenthwaite, near Keswick T01697-478325. With 20 beds in the middle of nowhere beneath the summit of Skiddaw.
£ **Thirlmere Hostel**, Old School, Stanah Cross, near Keswick, T01768-773224. Basic hostel with 28 beds in an old schoolhouse.

Camping
Syke Farm Camping Ground, Buttermere, T01768-770222. Basic campsite in idyllic countryside.

Ullswater *p33*
££££ **Sharrow Bay Country House Hotel**, T01768-486301, www.sharrowbay.co.uk. A luxury country hotel on the lake shore with a Michelin-starred restaurant. 26 bedrooms in 4 different locations near the lake.
£££ **Howtown Hotel**, Howtown, on Ullswater, T01768-486514, www.howtownhotel.co.uk. Open Apr-Sep. Traditional friendly hotel in a fabulous position on the southern shore of the lake. Also self-catering cottages.

££ Netherdene Guest House, Troutbeck, T01768-483475, www.netherdene.co.uk. Traditional Lakeland country house, great views, rooms with en suite facilities.

£ Helvellyn YHA, Greenside, Glenridding, T01768-482269. With 64 beds at 900 ft, base camp for the mountain above Ullswater.

£ Patterdale YHA, Patterdale, T01768-482394. With 82 beds in a Scandinavian-looking building.

Camping

Camping Barn, Swirral, on the Helvyllyn Range, near the routes to Striding Edge and Ullswater. Sleeps 8.

Side Farm Campsite, Patterdale, T01768-482237. Popular campsite in a stunning lakeside location.

The Lune and Eden Valleys *p34*

££££ Augill Castle, South Stainmore, near Kirkby Stephen, T01768-341937, www.stayinacastle.com. Wonderfully converted old castle with friendly hosts, fluffy towels in the bathrooms and happy breakfast atmosphere in the old dining room.

£££ Hipping Hall, Cowan Bridge, Kirkby Lonsdale, T01524-271187, www.hippinghall.com. Very pleasant country house hotel just outside Kirkby Lonsdale, good for exploring the Lune Valley.

£££ Tufton Arms Hotel, Market Sq, Appleby, T01768-351593, www.tuftonarmshotel.co.uk. Rambling old hotel right in the middle of town, with good-value lunchtime snacks, comfortable rooms and conservatory restaurant.

£££-££ Black Swan Hotel, Ravenstonedale, near Kirkby Stephen, T01539-623204, www.blackswanhotel.com. Privately owned, comfortable hotel in a Victorian building in the middle of a quiet village.

££ Bongate House, Bongate, Appleby, T01768-351245. A large family-run guesthouse in a fine Georgian building on the northern edge of town.

££ Ing Hill Lodge, Mallerstang Dale, near Kirkby Stephen, T01768-371153. Georgian house with a warm welcome in a beautiful position not far from Pendragon Castle.

££ Royal Oak, Bongate, Appleby, T01768-351463. The best bet for staying above a pub, does good and imaginative pub food freshly prepared daily.

££-£ Croglin Castle Hotel, South Rd, Kirkby Stephen, T01768-371389. Decent pub hotel with good food, convenient for the station.

£ Bents Camping Barn T01768-371760 or T01539-623681. £4 per person per night, £48 for sole use, with 12 beds. A 17th-century barn on the edge of the Howgill Fells, 5 miles from Kirkby Stephen railway station, on the Coast to Coast walk.

£ Kirkby Stephen Hostel, Market St, Kirkby Stephen, T01768-371793, www.kirkbystephenhostel.co.uk. Right in the middle of town, 1.5 miles from the station, in a converted chapel with 44 beds in 2-, 4-, 6- and 8-bed rooms.

The Cumbrian coast *p37*

££££-£££ Winder Hall Country House, Lorton, near Cockermouth, T01900-85107, www.winderhall.co.uk. An ancient manor house hotel with a lovely garden, hot tub and jacuzzi.

£££ Aynsome Manor Hotel, Cartmel, T01539-536653, www.aynsomemanorhotel.co.uk. A small family-run country house hotel, cosy and wood-panelled with glorious views from the garden and good food in the quiet restaurant.

£££ Brookhouse Inn, Boot, T01946-723288, www.brookhouseinn.co.uk. On the Eskdale Green to Hard Knott road. A popular choice with walkers.

£££ The Pheasant Inn, Bassenthwaite Lake, Cockermouth, T01768-776234, www.the-pheasant.co.uk. 15th-century coaching inn with cosy fires, comfortable rooms, fine dining and real ales.

£££-££ Cavendish Arms, Cartmel, T01539-536240, www.thecavendisharms.co.uk. An old locals' pub with character in the middle of the village, fine real ales (including their own brew) and a back garden.

£££-££ Masons Arms, Strawberry Bank, Cartmel Fell, T01539-568486, www.masonsarmsstrawberrybank.co.uk. A very popular own-brew pub with comfortable good value rooms, reliable food and views all around. Recommended.

£££-££ Netherwood, Lindale Rd, Grange-over-Sands, T01539-532552, www.netherwood-hotel.co.uk. Another grand old country house, Victorian, with views over Morecambe Bay.

££ Church Walk House, Church Walk, Ulverston, T01229-582211, www.church walkhouse.co.uk. A charming, central B&B.

££ Dale View B&B, Boot, T01946-723236, www.booteskdale.co.uk. B&B in the old Post Office.

££ Holly House Hotel, Main St, Ravenglass, T01229-717230. A centrally located hotel with reasonable food.

£ Eskdale YHA, T01946-723219. The local youth hostel.

Camping

Hollins Farm Campsite, at the other end of the Esk valley, in Boot, T01946-723253. Idyllic pitches for about £5 a night.

Turner Hall Farm, Seathwaite, Duddon Valley, T01229-716420. Camping for about £5 a night per pitch.

⑦ Restaurants

Kendal and around *p24*
££ New Moon, 129 Highgate, T01539-729254, www.newmoonrestaurant.co.uk. A long-standing local favourite offering modern European cooking in a civilized environment.

££ Punchbowl Inn, Crosthwaite, Lyth Valley, T01539-568237, www.the-punchbowl.co.uk. Contemporary formal restaurant or traditional pub menu.

££-£ Déjà Vu, 124 Stricklandgate, T01539-724843, www.dejavukendal.com. A small French restaurant doing vegetarian and Spanish evenings as well. Booking essential at the weekends.

££-£ Paulo Gianni's, 21a Stramongate, T01539-725858, www.paulogiannis.co.uk. Popular local Italian with good pizzas and pasta as well as daily specials of Mediterranean food.

£ Chang Thai, 54 Stramongate, T01539-720387, www.changthaikendal.co.uk. The only Thai restaurant in Kendal, very laid-back and reasonably priced.

£ Eastern Balti, 22 Wildman St, T01539-724074, www.easternbalti.webs.com. Kendal's first Balti House, doing fine Indian cooking in elegant surroundings with a comprehensive vegetarian menu, and a takeaway service.

£ Low Sizergh Barn, Sizergh, T01539-560426, www.lowsizerghbarn.co.uk. Traditional tea rooms and farm shop.

Windermere and Bowness *p25*
Foodies will be spoilt for choice with some fantastic gastro restaurants in the area.
£££ Holbeck Ghyll, Holbeck Lane, between Windermere and Ambleside, T01539-432375, www.holbeckghyll.com. Michelin-starred restaurant, extensive wine list, lovely views.

£££ Linthwaite House, Crook Rd, Bowness-on-Windermere, T15394-88600, www.linthwaite.com. Award-winning restaurant, one of the best in the Lakes, serving modern British food.

£££ Miller Howe, Rayrigg Rd, Windermere, T01539-442536, www.millerhowe.com. Great views over the lake and fells as you dine.

£££ The Samling, Ambleside Rd, Windermere, T01539 431922, www.the samlinghotel.co.uk. Fine dining in a boutique hotel.

£££-££ Cedar Manor, Ambleside Rd, Windermere, T01539-443192, www.cedarmanor.co.uk. Elegant fine dining using fresh local ingredients.

££ Francine's, 27 Main Rd, T01539-444088, www.francinesrestaurantwindermere.co.uk. Relaxed bistro-style restaurant and café specializing in seafood. Great wine list.

££ Jericho's, Birch St, T01539-4442522, www.jerichos.co.uk. Sat only. Well-prepared modern British food in the middle of town. Limited seasonal menu.

££-£ Angel Inn, Helm Rd, Bowness-on-Windermere, T01539-444080, www.theangelinnbowness.com. Traditional inn with a modern twist.

££-£ Postilion Restaurant, Ash St, Bowness-on-Windermere, T01539-445852, www.postilionrestaurant.co.uk. A traditional British and continental restaurant, home-made food with fine wine selection.

***

Ambleside and around *p28*

£££ Drunken Duck Inn, Barngates, T01539-436347, www.drunkenduckinn.co.uk. Lunch, dinner or afternoon tea using high-quality local ingredients.

££ Lucy's on a Plate, Church St, Ambleside, T01539-431191, www.lucysofambleside. co.uk. Café, restaurant and cookery school with a relaxed atmosphere. Eclectic fare.

££ The Queen's Head, Townhead, Troutbeck, T01539-432174, www.queensheadtroutbeck.co.uk. A 17th-century inn with excellent food.

££ Sheila's Cottage, The Slack, Ambleside, T01539-433079, www.sheilascottage.co.uk. Quaint restaurant and tea rooms serving simple English food.

££ Zeffirelli's, Compston Rd, Ambleside, T01539-433845, www.zeffirellis.com. Wholesome wholefood pizzeria unusually enough with a 2-screen cinema attached, right in the village centre.

££-£ Glass House, Rydal Rd, T01539-432137, www.theglasshouserestaurant.co.uk. Modern imaginative menu and decor in a lovely setting, unfussy and reasonably priced.

££-£ Mr Dodds Restaurant, Rydal Rd, Ambleside, T01539-432134, www.dodds restaurant.co.uk. Morning coffee, lunch or evening menu, vegetarian dishes, pizza to eat in or take-away.

££-£ Tarantella, 10 Lake Rd, Ambleside, www.tarantellarestaurant.co.uk. Modern Italian-style restaurant.

£ Apple Pie, Rydal Rd, Ambleside, T01539-433679, www.applepieambleside.co.uk. Excellent home-made cakes, breads and sandwiches in this popular little café.

***

Grasmere *p28*

£££ Rothay Garden Hotel, Grasmere, T01539-435334 www.rothaygarden.com. Conservatory restaurant, quality food and professional service.

£££-££ Lancrigg Country House Hotel, Easedale Rd, T01539-435317, www.lancrigg.co.uk. A particularly good vegetarian restaurant, snuggled into the Easedale Valley.

££ Oak Bank Hotel, Broadgate, Grasmere, T01539-435217, www.lakedistricthotel.co.uk. Fine dining and attention to detail.

££-£ Jumble Room Café, Grasmere, T01539-435188, www.thejumbleroom.co.uk. A cheerful place for filling British food.

***

Keswick and around *p31*

£££-££ Cottage in the Wood, Whinlatter Forest, T01768-778409, www.thecottage inthewood.co.uk. Uses local breeds of pig, sheep and cattle as well as wild mushrooms, nettles and wild garlic in their menu.

££ Morrel's, 34 Lake Rd, T01768-772666. Well-respected traditional British restaurant on the road down to the theatre, plenty of vegetarian options. Weekend booking essential.

££-£ Luca's Greta Bridge, High Hill, T01768-774621, www.lucasristorante.co.uk. Popular local Italian restaurant, family-owned and run, with home-made pizzas and pastas, as well as steaks, fish and vegetarian menu.

The Lune and Eden Valleys *p34*
£££-££ Appleby Manor Country House, Roman Rd, Appleby, T01768-351571, www.applebymanor.co.uk. Choose from a local menu that includes Lancashire duckling, Cumbrian venison or Arnside plaice.
££ Sun Inn, 6 Market St, Kirkby Lonsdale, T015242 71965, www.sun-inn.info. 17th-century inn with a small intimate restaurant or dining at the bar.
££ Tufton Arms, Market Square, Appleby, T01768-351593, www.tuftonarms hotel.co.uk. Long-standing reputation for its conservatory restaurant serving classic dishes with a modern twist.
££-£ Royal Oak, Bongate, Appleby, T01768-351463, www.royaloakappleby.co.uk. Good imaginative pub food, freshly prepared daily.
£ Costas Tapas Bar, 9 Queen St, Penrith, T01768-866987, www.costastapasbar.co.uk. Delivers a shot of sunny Spain in the centre of town, with authentic snacks.
£ Croglin Castle Hotel, Kirkby Stephen, T01768-371389, www.croglincastleand brewery.co.uk. Small restaurant offering a good modern British menu.
£ Riverside Fish and Chips, Sands, Appleby, T01768-351464. Serves up the national dish for lunch and supper to eat-in or take-away beside the River Eden.

The Cumbrian coast *p37*
£££-££ Eden Lodge, Conishead Grange, Coast Rd, Bardsea, T01229-587067, www.eden-lodge.com. Elegant but unpretentious. Classic British menu.
£££-££ Hare and Hounds, Bowland Bridge, Grange-over-Sands, T01539-568333, www.hareandhoundsbowlandbridge.co.uk. Inspired seasonal menu.

£££-££ Netherwood Hotel, Lindale Rd, Grange-over-Sands, T01539-532552, www.netherwood-hotel.co.uk. Daily changing menu such as Lakeland lamb, beef, venison and Gressingham Duck.
££ Quince and Medlar, 13 Castlegate, Cockermouth, T01900-823579, www.quinceandmedlar.co.uk. A candlelit top-class vegetarian restaurant.
££ Zest Low Rd, on the outskirts of Whitehaven, T01946-692848, www.zestwhitehaven.com. Accomplished modern British menu including grilled Cumbrian steaks and fresh seafood. Also runs **Zest Harbourside** café-bar.

🎵 Pubs and bars

Ambleside and around *p27*
Golden Rule, Smithy Brow, Ambleside, T01539-432257. A very good pub popular with walkers and pulling some fine real ales. No hot food but great pork pies.
Lucy 4, 2 St Mary's La, T01539-434666. A tapas wine bar with a good atmosphere.

Grasmere *p28*
Tweedies Bar, Red Bank Rd, T01539-435300 www.tweediesbargrasmere.co.uk. Award-winning pub with a great range of beers and scrumpy. Live music.

The Cumbrian coast *p37*
Blacksmith's Arms, Broughton Mills, just outside Broughton in the lovely Lickie Valley, T01229-716824. A locals' pub hidden away, with a very ancient interior but reliable food.

🎭 Entertainment

Keswick *p31*
Alhambra Cinema, St John's St, with interesting screenings of mainstream and arthouse films by the Keswick Film Club, T01768-772398, www.keswickfilmclub.org.

Theatre by the Lake, Lakeside, Keswick T01768-774411, www.theatrebythelake.com. Middle-scale touring productions at one of the most prettily situated theatres in the UK.

The Lune and Eden Valleys *p34*
Upfront Gallery and Puppet Theatre, near Hutton-in-the-Forest, T01768-484538, www.up-front.com. Changing exhibitions and performances. Also has a vegetarian restaurant on site.

❂ Festivals

Windermere *p25*
Sep Bowness Theatre Festival. Hosted by the Old Laundry each year from mid-Sep to Oct, www.oldlaundrytheatre.com or find details from *The World of Beatrix Potter*, which usually features some top names in performance, with poetry readings, films and interesting talks.

The Lune and Eden Valleys *p34*
Jun Appleby Horse Fair is a traditional gypsy horse fair. See the ponies being washed in the Eden ready for sale.

▲ What to do

There's a huge variety of activities on offer from hot air ballooning and parachuting to mountaineering or pony trekking. The visitor information centres can provide further details.

Boat trips
As well as cruising on the lake, it's also possible to hire your own boat and have your own *Swallows and Amazons* adventure (see Watersports, below).
Coniston Launch, T01768-775753, www.conistonlaunch.co.uk. Boat trips on Coniston Water (see page 30).
Keswick Launch, T01768-772263, www.keswick-launch.co.uk. Cruises on Derwentwater (see page 32).

Steam Yacht Gondola, T01539-432733, www.national trust.org.uk/gondola. Cruise around Coniston Water in style on this unique yacht, rebuilt from the original Victorian *Gondola*, launched in 1850 (see page 30).
Ullswater Steamers, T01768-482229, www.ullswater-steamers.co.uk. Heritage cruises the length of the lake from Pooley Bridge to Glenridding (see page 33).
Windermere Lake Cruises, T01539-443360, www.windermere-lakecruises.co.uk. 45-min to 3-hr trips across Lake Windermere to Lakeside, Bowness and Ambleside (see page 25).

Climbing
A number of companies offer rock climbing and mountaineering; see the multi-activities section, below. Also contact the **Fell and Rock Climbing Club**, www.frcc.co.uk, which publishes a climbing guide and routes.
Ambleside Climbing Wall, 101 Lake Rd, in **Adventure Peaks** shop, T01539-433794 www.adventurepeaks.com/climbing-wall. Open Mon-Fri 1000-2130, Sat-Sun 1000-1900.
Go Ape, Grizedale Forest Park, T0845-6439215, www.goape.co.uk/days-out/grizedale. Tree-top adventure using high ropes and zip wires.
Highpoint Mountain Guides, T01539-437691 www.mountainguides.co.uk. Specialist company that provides experienced guides for hiking, rock climbing or scrambling and runs courses on navigation and winter skills.
Keswick Climbing Wall, Keswick, T01768-772000, www.keswickclimbingwall.co.uk. Challenging climbing wall and outdoor activity centre. Lessons available.
Lakeland Climbing Centre, near Kendal, T01539-721766, www.kendalwall.co.uk. Wide range of indoor and outdoor climbing courses.
Tree Top Trek, Brockhole, Lake District Visitor Centre, T01539-447186, www.treetoptrek.co.uk. Swing, climb, balance

and fly your way through the ancient woodland canopy.

Via Ferrata & Zip, Honister Slate Mine (see page 33). Scale the sheer rock face of the old miners' route using fixed cables then sail down on the zip wire.

Cycling

Both road cycling and mountain biking are a popular activity in the Lakes. The **Cumbria Cycleway** runs through Kirkby Lonsdale, Sedbergh, Garsdale, Kirkby Stephen and Appleby. Details from TICs. The **Yorkshire Dales Cycleway** passes through Dent. **Windermere Lake Cruises** (see Boat trips) runs a Cross-Lakes Shuttlebus service which will transport bikes, call in advance. See also Getting around, page 19.

A useful book is *Lake District Mountain Biking* by Chris Gore and Richard Staton. The website www.mountain-bike-cumbria.co.uk is also useful.

Askew Cycles, Old Brewery, Wildman St, Kendal, T01539-728057, www.askewcycles.co.uk.

Bike Treks, Rydal Rd, Ambleside, T01539-431245, www.bike-treks.co.uk. Cycle centre and shop offering route advice and bike hire.

Country Lanes, Windermere train station, T01539-444544, www.countrylands district.co.uk. Bike hire, cycle tour packages and boat trips combined with bike hire. You can take a cruiser to Lakeside at the southern tip of Windermere where 2-hr cycle routes links the villages of Finsthwaite and Newby Bridge, or follow the River Leven (and steam train) to Haverthwaite.

Cyclewise Whinlatter, Whinlatter Forest Park, T01768 898775, www.cyclewise.co.uk. Bike hire and training.

Electric Bicycle Network, www.electric bicyclenetwork.com. For those that prefer to take things are little easier, the website provides details of hire (£20-30 per day) and charge points around the Lakes.

Ghyllside Cycles, Market Cross, Ambleside, www.ghyllside.co.uk. Cycle shop.

Gone Mountain Biking, Kinniside Portinscale, Keswick T01768-780812, www.gonemountainbiking.co.uk. Bike hire and organized trips.

Keswick Mountain Bikes, Southey Hill, Keswick T01768-775202, www.keswick mountainbikes.co.uk. Shop and cycle hire.

Lakeland Pedlar, Bicycle Centre and Wholefood Café, Henderson Yard, Keswick, T01768-775752, www.lakelandpedlar.co.uk.

Wheelbase, Mill Yard, Staveley, Kendal, T01539-821443, www.wheelbase.co.uk. The UK's largest bike store, a good place to stock up on equipment.

Fishing

Permits for fishing in respective areas of the Lake District can be obtained from Ambleside, Kendal and Windermere visitor centres, as well as **Carlson's Fishing Tackle Shop**, Kirkland, Kendal, T01539-724867, or **Kendal Sports**, 30 Stramongate, Kendal, T01539-721554, and **Fishing Hut**, The Boulevard, Windermere Rd, Grange-over-Sands, T01539-532854. These places can also provide maps and other useful information showing where fishing is allowed. Or consult www.lakedistrictfishing.net. Around the Lune Valley, day permits from **Pigneys**, Appleby, T01768-351240, or in Kirkby Lonsdale from TIC. In Kirkby Stephen from **WAS Kilvington**, Market Sq, T01768-371495. In Sedbergh, tickets from the TIC. Mar-Aug £10 day.

Horse riding

Also see also multi activities, below.
Crooked Birch Equestrian Centre, Subberthwaite, near Ulverston, T01229-885060, www.crookedbirch.co.uk.
Cumbrian Heavy Horses, Chappels Farm, Whicham Valley, near Millom, T01229-777764, www.cumbrianheavyhorses.com.

Hipshow Riding Stables, Hipshow Farm, Mealbank, near Kendal, T01539-728221, www.horseridingholidays.co.uk.
Lakeland Equestrian, Wynlass Beck Stables, Windermere, T01539-443811, www.lakelandequestrian.com.
Lakeland Pack Pony Holidays, Moss Side Farm, Woodland, Broughton-in-Furness, T01229 716947, www.lakelandpack ponies.co.uk.
Park Foot Trekking Centre, Howtown, Pooley Bridge, T01768-486696.
Stonetrail Holidays, Street Farm, Raven-stonedale, Kirkby Stephen, T01539-623444, www.stonetrailridingcentre.com.

Multi-activities

The following companies off a range of activities such as abseiling, archery, canoeing, ghyll and gorge scrambling, kayaking, mountain biking, orienteering, ridge walking, raft building, rock climbing and wild camping.
Adventures, 6 Riverside Terrace, Cockermouth, T01900-829775, www.adventures.org.uk.
Joint Adventures, Coniston, T01539-441526, www.jointadventures.co.uk.
Keswick Adventure Centre, Brundholme Rd, Keswick, T01768-775687, www.keswick adventurecentre.co.uk.
Lakeland Mountain Ventures, Kendal, T01539-741318, www.lakelandmountain ventures.co.uk.
Mere Mountains, Windermere, T01539-535030, www.meremountains.co.uk.
Newlands Adventure Centre, Stair, near Keswick, T01768-778463, www.activity-centre.com.
River Deep Mountain High, Low Wood, near Ulverston, T01539-531116, www.riverdeepmountainhigh.co.uk.
Rookin House Equestrian and Activity Centre, Troutbeck, T01768-483561, www.rookinhouse.co.uk.
Summitreks, 14 Yewdale Rd, Coniston, T01539-441212. www.summitreks.co.uk.

Paragliding
Air Ventures, T07830 281986, www.airventures.co.uk.
Sunsoar Paragliding, South Rd, Kirkby Stephen, T01768-371021, www.sunsoar-paragliding.com.
Tandem Paragliding, Keswick, T01768-771442, www.keswickparagliding.com.

Sightseeing and specialist tours
Lake District Tours, T01539-552103, www.lakedistricttours.co.uk. Half- and full-day sightseeing tours, with an emphasis on nature and hiking.
Lakes Supertours, T01539-442751, www.lakes-supertours.com. Specializes in half-day and full-day tours in 16-seater mini-coaches, including literary tours taking in sights associated with Wordsworth, Ruskin, Beatrix Potter and Arthur Ransome.
Mountain Goat, T01539-445161, www.mountain-goat.com. Provides holidays and half- and full-day sightseeing tours of the Lake District. Itineraries include the Beatrix Potter Experience, a short break focusing on the various locations associated with Potter's life and stories.

Volunteering
Contact the **British Trust for Conservation Volunteers**, Brockhole, Windermere, T01539-443098, www.btcv.org.uk, if you'd like to lend a hand maintaining the Lake Districts crumbling enclosure walls, footpaths, plant trees or cut back rhododendrons.

Walking
The **National Park Authority** publishes a free annual *Events and Parklife* magazine (available from most TICs) with details of guided walks and other events throughout the year. The **Ramblers Association**, www.ramblers.com, has details of routes, and Andrew Leaney's website, www.leaney.org, is a useful photographic guide. Walking tours for individuals in groups are also organized by:

Brathay Exploration Group Trust, Brathay Hall, Ambleside, T01539-433942; www.brathayexploration.org.uk;
Contours Walking Holidays, T10629-821900, www.contours.co.uk;
Cumbria Outdoors, Hawsend Centre, Portinscale, Keswick, T01768-772816, www.cumbriaoutdoors.com;
Lakeland Walking Breaks, Keswick, T01768-773610, www.lakeland-walking-breaks.co.uk.

Long-distance paths across the Lake District include the 70-mile Cumbria Way from Ulverston to Carlisle, and the first part of Wainwright's Coast-to-Coast walk from St Bee's Head to Robin Hood Bay.

The area around the Lune and Eden Valleys abounds in way-marked walks, a selection below, but many of the fells are open access too. The **Alternative Pennine Way** runs through Kirkby Stephen and Appleby, more interesting than the National Trail, details from Kirkby TIC; the **Eden Way** long-distance walk begins at Rockcliffe Marsh and ends at Mallerstang along the course of the river; **Westmorland Heritage Walk** traces the boundaries of the old county, passing through Kirkby Lonsdale, Sedbergh, Mallerstang and Appleby; **Lady Anne's Way** runs for 100 miles from Skipton to Penrith along the route ridden by the elderly Lady Anne as she restored her 6 castles; **Dales Way** (from Ilkley to Bowness-on-Windermere) passes through Sedbergh, Dent and Lea Yeat (guides are available from Kirkby Lonsdale or Sedbergh TIC).

Watersports
Coniston Boating Centre, Coniston, T01539-441366, www.lake-district.gov.uk. Plot a course for Wild Cat Island of *Swallows and Amazons* fame. RYA sailing courses, electric motor boats, dinghies, rowing boats and canoes for hire.

Derwentwater Marina, Portinscale, T01768-772912, www.derwentwater marina.co.uk. RYA sailing courses.
Lakeland Boat Hire, Pooley Bridge, T01768-486800, www.landlandboathire.co.uk. Hire canoes or kayaks.
Lakes Leisure Windermere, Rayrigg Rd, Windermere, T01539-447183, www.lakesleisure.org.uk/windermere. Canoeing sailing and windsurfing courses and multi-activity days.
Low Wood Watersports, Windermere, T01539-439441, www.englishlakes.co.uk/watersports. Sailing, canoeing tuition and rental, plus rowing boats, motor boats and water skiing.
Platty+, Lodore Boat Landing, Derwentwater, T01768-776572, www.platty plus.co.uk. RYA courses, dinghy and canoe hire, plus a chance to sail in a replica Viking long ship or paddle a dragon boat.
Windermere Canoe, Bowness-on-Windermere, T01539-444451, www.windermerecanoekayak.com. Kayak and canoe hire from £30 a day.

⊖ Transport

Stagecoach Cumbria, www.stagecoach bus.com, operates a network of rambler bus services including the following routes:
77 Keswick–Portinscale–Grange–Seatoller–Honister Slate Mine–Buttermere–Whinlatter Forest Visitor Centre– Keswick; **108** Penrith–Pooley Bridge–Aira Force–Glenridding–Patterdale; **505** Kendal–Windermere–Ambleside–Hawkshead (for Tarn Hows)–Waterhead (for Coniston boat services)–Coniston; **516** Ambleside–Skelwith Bridge–Elterwater– Chapel Stile–Dungeon Ghyll; **517** Bowness Pier–Windermere–Kirkstone Pass–Brothers Water–Patterdale–Glenridding; **555** Kendal–Windermere–Brockhole National Park Centre–Ambleside–Grasmere–Keswick.

Hadrian's Wall

Built by the Romans and their slaves, Hadrian's Wall marked the northern boundary of their empire in the second and third centuries AD and was their most impressive engineering achievement in Northern Europe. Strategic considerations at the time of its construction mean that the route it takes still commands some of the best views between Carlisle and Newcastle.

Carlisle advertises itself as a 'great border city' with some justification. This strategic town near the mouth of the River Eden was continually at the centre of border disputes right up to the rebellion of Bonnie Prince Charlie in 1745. Today it's the county town of Cumbria and still a fairly forbidding place despite a clutch of attractions worth an afternoon of anyone's time: the cathedral, castle and local museum and art gallery called Tullies House. Stretching away to the east of Carlisle and really the best reason for a visit to the city, the World Heritage Site of Hadrian's Wall is a crumbling relic, 73 miles long, still standing up to six of its original 10 feet in some places, hugging the high ground all the way to Newcastle. The most complete remains of forts are at Birdoswald, Housesteads and Chesters, with a superb stretch of the wall itself near Walltown Crags. Hexham is a good-looking abbey town close to the wall above the river Tyne. Further east, Newcastle upon Tyne is the most vigorous city in the North, thanks to its wealth of new developments and optimistic, forward-looking spirit born out of industrial decline.

Arriving at Hadrian's Wall

Getting there Carlisle is on the main east coast **train** line to Glasgow from London Euston. A branch line runs to Brampton, Haltwhistle, Reburn, Haydon Bridge, Hexham and Newcastle. The Leeds–Settle–Carlisle railway is easily the most scenic route to the city, www.settle-carslisle.co.uk. **Virgin** trains serve Carlisle direct from London Euston (three hours 40 minutes) or more frequently with a change at Preston (4½ hours). Carlisle is at the top of the M6 motorway, a little over 300 miles from London, about five hours' drive. Hadrian's Wall is easily reached along the impressive A69 to Newcastle upon Tyne (46 miles to the east). Most of the major Roman sites are reached along the B6318, a minor road following the course of the one built by General Wade to suppress the Scots under Oliver Cromwell. **National Express** ① *T08705-808080, www.nationalexpress.co.uk*, runs two coaches to Carlisle from London Victoria at 0930 and 1030 arriving at 1610 and 1745 respectively, as well as a nightcoach leaving at 2230 arriving at 0505. Coaches also run from Carlisle to Leeds, Manchester and Birmingham. ▸▸ *See Transport, page 69.*

Getting around The centre of Carlisle is easily small enough to be explored on foot. Buses to Hadrian's Wall leave from Warwick Road and the bus station on Lonsdale Street. **Hadrian's Wall Bus**, run by **Stagecoach** in Cumbria ① *T01434-322002, www.hadrians-wall.org*, runs from Easter to October and links Carlisle with Hexham, Haltwhistle, Brampton and most of the main Roman sites; it can carry two bicycles free of charge. By train, the **Tyne Valley Line** to Newcastle from Carlisle calls at Brampton, Haltwhistle, Bardon Mill and Haydon Bridge.

Tourist information Carlisle Visitor Centre ① *Old Town Hall, T01228-625600, www.discovercarlisle.co.uk, Mar-Jun, Sep-Oct Mon-Sat 0930-1700, Jul-Aug also open Sun 1030-1600, Nov-Feb Mon-Sat 1000-1600*, has details of cycle routes, bike hire and accommodation. **Haltwhistle TIC** ① *Mechanics Institute, Westgate, T01434 322002, Mar-Nov daily 1000-1630.* **Hexham TIC** ① *Wentworth Car Park, T01434-652220, Apr-Oct Mon-Sat 0930-1700, Sun 1100-1600, Nov-Mar Mon-Sat 1000-1630.*

Carlisle → *For listings, see pages 64-69.*

From Court Square in front of the train station, the round towers of the 19th-century **Citadel**, modelled on a gate erected by Henry VIII, make an imposing entrance to the town centre down English Street. A further 100 yds down, this pedestrianized area opens out into the market square. The cross from which Bonnie Prince Charlie proclaimed his father king still stands, as does the Elizabethan town hall, now home to the helpful Carlisle Visitor Centre. Next door is the **Guildhall** ① *T01228-534781, contact Tullie House Museum, see below, for opening times*, which has a small museum on the history of the building, dating from 1405.

To the left of the Guildhall, Castle Street heads down past the cathedral to the Tullie House Museum, and then over the new Irishgate footbridge or under the subway to the castle itself. **Carlisle Cathedral** ① *7 Abbey St, T01228-548151, www.carlislecathedral.org.uk, Mon-Sat 0730-1815, Sun 0730-1700, guides available, suggested donation £5, Prior's Kitchen restaurant in the medieval undercroft of the fratry (see Restaurants, page 66)*, is largely a 19th-century concoction although a fair amount of the medieval building survives. Built out of distinctive red sandstone, highlights of the interior include the East Window with its 14th-century stained glass images of the Last Judgement in the tracery lights, and the Brougham Triptych: a carved Flemish altarpiece depicting the Passion in St Wilfrid's Chapel. The choir has a 14th-century barrel-vaulted ceiling and beautifully carved capitals on its columns representing the labours of the months of the year. The choir stalls provide more fine examples of medieval carving. Early 16th-century paintings in the north and south aisles on the back of the choir stalls tell the stories of St Cuthbert and St Anthony. There's also a gift shop in the cathedral and good value food in the atmospheric vaults of the Prior's Kitchen.

Just down the road from the cathedral, the **Tullie House Museum** ① *Castle St, T01228-618718, www.tulliehouse.co.uk, Apr-Oct Mon-Sat 1000-1700, Sun 1100-1700, Nov-Mar Mon-Sat 1000-1700, Sun 1200-1700, £7, children free, tickets valid for a full year*, is an award-winning local history museum and art gallery. Vivid and imaginative interactive displays trace the history of the city from the Romans to the present day, a place where visitors are encouraged to 'come face to face with the people who lived, loved, fought and died for this part of Britain over the last ten thousand years'. As well as a reconstruction of part of Hadrian's Wall, there's a particularly strong section on the Border Reivers, the lawless families that terrorized this part of Britain for centuries.

Carlisle Castle ① *(EH), Castle Way, T01228-591922, Apr-Sep daily 0930-1800, Oct daily 1000-1700, Nov-Mar weekends only 1000-1600, £5.60, children £3.30*, was built on the site of a Roman fort, between the natural barriers of the rivers Eden and Caldew, to defend the western end of the border with Scotland. Many of the remains still standing today, including the massive keep, date from the 12th century, constructed under the orders of Henry I. The keep contains an exhibition on the last time the castle saw action, when it served as the prison for captured Jacobites after Charles Stuart's unsuccessful attempt on the throne in 1747. The castle is also home to the military museum of the King's Own Royal Border Regiment. Great views from the castle walls.

East along Hadrian's Wall → For listings, see pages 64-69.

Hadrian's Wall was built by order of the Emperor Hadrian following his visit to Britain in AD 122. It was planned as a continuous wall with a castle every Roman mile and two turrets between each castle, running some 80 miles from Maia (Bowness-on-Solway) past Luguvalium (Carlisle) to Segedunum (Newcastle upon Tyne). A new 81-mile National Trail now follows its entire length, through some of the bleakest landscape in Britain. The wall itself survives most visibly east of Birdoswald and west of Chesters along the military road built by General Wade, now the B6318.

At **Birdoswald Roman Fort** ① *(EH), T01697-747602, Mar-Oct daily 1000-1730 (last admission 1700), Nov-Feb exterior only, £5.20, children £3.30*, the remains include a unique drill hall or basilica as well as the outline of granary buildings, at what was once a large fort designed for 1000 legionaries. The masonry of the fort's west gate is particularly impressive. There's also an interactive visitor centre.

Close to the old village of Brampton, just before Birdoswald, the **Banks East Turret** and **Pike Hill Signal Tower** are both well preserved. They can be reached beyond the atmospheric remains of a 12th-century **Lanercost Augustinian Priory** ① *(EH)*,

T01697-73030, Apr-Sep daily 1000-1800, Oct daily 1000-1700, £3.40, children £2. One mile from Birdoswald, the mile-castle at **Poltross Burn**, Gilsland is in an exceptionally good state of repair.

At **Greenhead**, 'Gateway to Hadrian's Wall', the A69 becomes a spectacular road as it enters Northumberland, with distant views north and south over apparently endless wastes. The 400-m-long section of the wall at **Walltown Crags** is one of the most impressive: here it's still at least 7 ft wide and 5 ft high in places as it clings to the precipitous edge of the crags, including the remains of a turret.

Close to the Walltown Crags is the entertaining **Roman Army Museum** ⓘ *T01697-747485, www.vindolanda.com, Nov-Feb Sat-Sun 1000-1600, Feb-Mar and Oct daily 1000-1700, Mar-Sep daily 1000-1800, £5.25, children £3, £10/£5.50 with Vindolanda*, ideal for a rainy day. Exhibits include a Roman Army recruitment video, an Eagle's Eye View from a chopper along the wall, as well as some real Roman pottery amid the replicas of legionaries' uniforms and weaponry.

At Once Brewed, the **Northumberland National Park Visitor Centre** ⓘ *Military Rd, T01434-344396, Apr-Oct daily 0930-1700, Nov-Mar Sat-Sun 1000-1500*, provides information and walking leaflets on this central and most popular section of the wall. Within walking distance of the centre is **Vindolanda** ⓘ *T01434-344277, www.vindolanda.com, Apr-Sep daily 1000-1800, Nov-Feb 1000-1600, £6.50, children £4, £10/£5.50 with Roman Army Museum*, a recently excavated little civilian settlement, as well as an open-air museum featuring a reconstructed Roman temple, shop, house and croft.

Two and a half miles northeast of Bardon Mill on the B6318, **Housesteads Roman Fort** ⓘ *(EH and NT) T01434-344363, Apr-Sep daily 0930-1800, Oct daily 1000-1700, Nov-Mar daily 1000-1600, £6, children £3.60,* is the most complete of its type to survive in the UK. Four gates, the commandant's house, barracks, granaries, hospital and latrines can all be clearly discerned. Superb views from the site too.

Signposted off the A69 between Bardon Mill and Haydon Bridge is the Allen Banks Car Park. This provides access to an extensive stretch of National Trust ornamental and historic woodland, formerly the **Ridley Hall Estate**, along the banks of the River Allen, a tributary of the Tyne. Walks lead past abandoned 19th-century summerhouses to the medieval **Pele Tower** of Staward Peel, standing on a promontory above the gorge.

Half a mile west of Chollerford on the B6318, is one of the best-preserved examples of a cavalry fort, **Chesters Roman Fort** ⓘ *(EH), T01434-681379, Apr-Sep daily 0930-1800, Oct daily 1000-1700, Nov-Mar daily 1000-1600, £5.20, children £3.10,* featuring the remains of the barracks, bath-house and HQ. In a beautiful riverside setting, it overlooks the remains of the bridge that carried the wall over the Tyne. The **Clayton Collection** of the altars and sculptures found along the wall is also here.

Twenty miles west of Newcastle, **Hexham** is a dignified old town on the River Tyne blessed with a remarkable abbey church. The best approach by car is from the north and the A69, over an impressive bridge across the Tyne. The train station is on this side of town too and it's a short work up cobbled Hallgate (past the TIC) to the centre. The first sight as such is the **Old Gaol**, the oldest recorded one of its type in England, purpose-built in 1332. It now contains the interesting **Border History Museum** ⓘ *T01434-652349, www.tyne daleheritage.org, Apr-Oct daily 0930-1600, Nov, Feb, Mar Mon, Tue, Sat 0930-1600, £2, children £1, family £5*, where you can 'listen to the medieval punishment commentary, hear about cross-border marriages in 1587 and find out what a Pele tower is'. Next up is the **Moot Hall** (which sometimes holds craft fairs, contact the TIC for details) with a gateway into the main Market Place, with **Hexham Abbey** ① *T01434-602031, www.hexhamabbey.org.uk, daily 0930-1700, suggested donation £3*, on its far side, and an attractive public park behind. Founded in AD 674, the ruddy stoned old building dominates the town and contains rare Roman and Saxon carvings. One of the more remarkable commemorates a Roman standard bearer called Flavinus of the Cavalry Regiment of Petriana stationed on the wall, who died aged 25 during the first century AD. The Saxon crypt of St Wilfrid also survives.

Newcastle and Gateshead → *For listings, see pages 64-69.*

As Liverpool is to the Northwest, so Newcastle upon Tyne is to the Northeast: on the up and up. In a spectacular position above the Tyne River, the once coal-blackened and grimey hub has become an upbeat weekending destination for twenty-somethings thanks to injections of European and lottery cash, a vigorous nightlife and the energy of its citizens, known as Geordies. Entering the city from the south, first impressions are of the dramatic multilevel river crossings, including the famous mini prototype of Sydney Harbour bridge. The Quayside has been at the centre of radical redevelopment in the last 15 years and the opening of the Millennium Bridge, the BALTIC Centre for Contemporary Art and The Sage confirmed the boom along the riverside in Newcastle and its fiercely competitive neighbour on the south bank, Gateshead. Despite the recession, even the older parts of the city centre have been caught up in the wave of optimism sweeping the region. Some say it all started with the *Angel of the North*, a giant gliderman sculpture perched above the A1. The rusty red steel thing sings in the wind, a potent symbol of this once heavily industrialized corner of the UK's aspirations for a less gritty future.

Arriving in Newcastle upon Tyne
Getting there **Newcastle International Airport** ① *6 miles northwest of the city centre at Woolsington, T0191-214 4444, www.newcastleairport.com*, has direct flights from all over the UK, Europe and beyond. There's a 25-minute metro link into the city centre.

Newcastle Central Station is a main stop on the London–York–Edinburgh rail line and has regular connections with the Northwest and Scotland. Journey times are around three hours from London King's Cross and 1½ hours from Edinburgh.

Newcastle is on the A1, about 275 miles north of London, usually reached in 5½ hours on that road, sometimes less on the M1 via Leeds. The main bus stations are Eldon Square and Haymarket. **National Express** ① *T08705-808080, www.nationalexpress.co.uk*, runs coaches from most major towns and cities in the UK. The service from London runs five times a day and once at night, taking about seven hours. **Wright Bros** ① *T0191-277 8000, www.wrights coaches.co.uk*, connects Newcastle with Keswick in the Lake District via Alston.

Getting around Although the areas of most interest to visitors are within walking distance of each other, the **Tyne and Wear Metro** ① *www.nexus.org.uk/metro*, is a good-value quick and easy way to get around and runs all the way out to the coast. **Metro Day Saver** tickets cost £4.40 and allow unlimited travel on the metro, Shields Ferry and local rail services (Newcastle to Sunderland).

Rusty redeeming angel

Standing on top of a disused coalmine just off the A1 south of Gateshead, the *Angel of the North* has become the symbol of the Northeast's regeneration. It's the largest sculpture in Britain, a giant steel man with huge glider-like wings for arms. The artist, Antony Gormley has commented on the poetic resonance of its position, above a place where men once worked in the dark. He has said that "the effect of the piece is in the alertness, the awareness of space and the gesture of the wings – they are not flat, they're about 3.5 degrees forward and give a sense of embrace". Commissioned by Gateshead Council in 1994, the sculpture stands taller than four double decker buses, with its stiff outstretched wings almost as long as a jumbo's. It was made in three parts, of a special weather-resistant steel containing oxidising copper, designed to age to a rich, rusty red, and it cost almost a million pounds. Money well spent. It was completed in early 1998, the foundations involving 150 tonnes of concrete being poured into piles to root the sculpture in the solid rock 20 yards below. Transmission of the windloads along the ribs, down the body and into these foundations enable it to withstand winds of more than 100 miles per hour. As angels go, this one's as down-to-earth as they come.

Regular buses are operated by **Arriva** ⓘ *www.arrivabus.co.uk*, **Go North East** ⓘ *www.simplygo.com*, and **Stagecoach** ⓘ *www.stagecoachbus.com*. Look out for the bright yellow **QuayLink** buses, which run regularly across Newcastle, Gateshead and the Quayside, linking all the main attractions. For further information contact **Traveline** ⓘ *T0870-608 2608, www.travelinenortheast.info*, or visit www.nexus.org.uk/bus.

The **Shields Ferry** ⓘ *www.nexus.org.uk/ferry*, runs every half an hour across the mouth of the Tyne between North Shields and South Shields, taking seven minutes.

Tourist information **Newcastle-Gateshead Visitor Centre** ⓘ *Central Arcade, T0191-277 8000, www.newcastlegateshead.com, Mon-Sat 0930-1730, Sun 1000-1600*. **Gateshead Quays Visitor Centre** ⓘ *T0191-433 4699, www.gateshead-quays.com, Mon-Thu 0830-1700, Fri 0830-1630, Sat 1000-1700, Sun 1100-1700*. There are also information centres in Gateshead Central Library, South Shields, North Shields, Whitley Bay and Sunderland. The websites www.newcastle.gov.uk and www.gateshead.gov.uk have some useful visitor information.

Places in Newcastle upon Tyne

Newcastle **Central Station** is quite a sight in itself: a grand survival of the city's industrial heyday, with lavish Victorian waiting rooms that have been converted into salubrious bars. Its main entrance is on Neville Street, which is a 10-minute walk from most of the city's sights.

Close to the train station, however, are a couple of worthwhile sights. The award-winning **Life Science Centre** ⓘ *Times Sq, just off Westmorland Rd and Scotswood Rd, T0191-243 8223, www.centre-for-life.co.uk, Mon-Sat 1000-1800, Sun 1100-1800, £8.25, children £6.45*, brings learning to life with 4D motion rides, interactive screens, the North's largest planetarium and games broadly based on the subject that was once called biology. It's great for kids and adults alike and is based around a cutting-edge life science

Newcastle upon Tyne

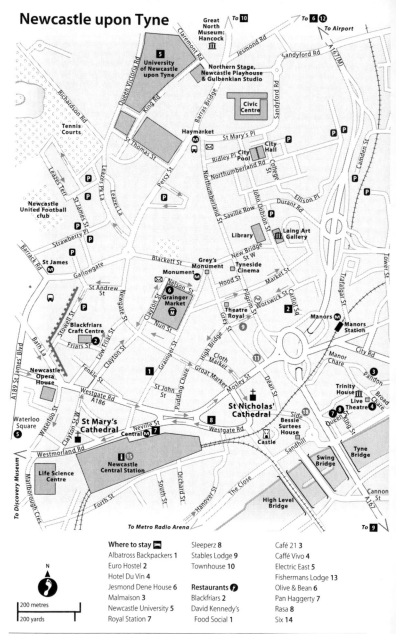

Where to stay 🛏
Albatross Backpackers **1**
Euro Hostel **2**
Hotel Du Vin **4**
Jesmond Dene House **6**
Malmaison **3**
Newcastle University **5**
Royal Station **7**

Sleeperz **8**
Stables Lodge **9**
Townhouse **10**

Restaurants 🍴
Blackfriars **2**
David Kennedy's
 Food Social **1**

Café 21 **3**
Caffé Vivo **4**
Electric East **5**
Fishermans Lodge **13**
Olive & Bean **6**
Pan Haggerty **7**
Rasa **8**
Six **14**

research institute. The place becomes an open-air ice rink in winter.

A 100 yards west, the aptly named **Discovery Museum** ① *Blandford Sq, T0191-232 6789, Mon-Sat 1000-1700, Sun 1400-1700, free*, is an interactive museum telling the story of Newcastle from the Romans to the present day. Filled with reconstructions, it offers the chance to re-enact the tales of its characters and includes the *Turbinia* display – built on the Tyne, she was the first ship to be powered by steam turbines and was the fastest of her time. In the Science Maze, there are hands-on demonstrations of scientific and engineering principles, including the waterpower inventions of celebrated Georgie William Armstrong.

A right turn out of the train station, leads past **St Nicholas' Cathedral** ① *T0191-232 1939*, formerly the Anglican parish church but with an impressive lantern tower, some interesting stained glass and a 15th-century brass memorial, commemorating Roger Thornton, thrice mayor of Newcastle, possibly the first of its type in the country. Next door, tucked beneath a railway arch, stands the keep built in the mid-12th century on the site of the Norman 'new' **castle** ① *Castle Keep, Castle Garth, St Nicholas St, T0191-232 7938, www.castlekeep-newcastle.org.uk, Mon-Sat 1000-1700, Sun 1200-1700, £4, under 18s free*, that gave the city its name a century earlier. Possibly also the original end point of Hadrian's Wall, the keep now stages changing exhibitions on its history.

From the castle the **High Level Bridge** takes both road and rail over the Tyne to Gateshead. Staying on the north bank, just above the Swing Bridge, **Bessie Surtees House** ① *(EH), access on the Quayside, T0191-269 1227, Mon-Fri 1000-1600, free*, consists of two buildings surviving from Tudor and Jacobean Newcastle. Now the regional offices of English Heritage, once

Northern accents

Although parodied by southerners as a succession of by gums, by 'eck and such like, the way people speak 'up North' is very finely differentiated. Within the space of any 20 square miles there are likely to be several different words for even the most common features of the local landscape. In Lancashire for example they call the hills 'fells', unlike the 'moors' of Yorkshire. Generally agreed upon across the region though are a 'beck' or stream, 'force' or waterfall, 'gill' or ravine, and 'tarn' or pond among many others mainly of Scandinavian origin. A law unto themselves are the Geordies. Regularly voted the most trustworthy telephone accent in the British Isles, Geordie is the native tongue of the citizens of Newcastle upon Tyne. Apparently the name, diminutive for George, dates back to the city's refusal to rise with the Northumbrian Jacobites in 1715 in support of the Old Pretender, would-be James III, against the new Hanoverian King George I. At its broadest, the accent can be quite incomprehensible to non-Geordies. Its peppered with 'Alreet' meaning Alright, and 'But' or 'Mon' used willy nilly at the end of sentences. A 'gadgie with a bottle of dog' translates as an old man with a bottle of Newcastle Brown Ale. Good luck trying to understand him.

the homes of wealthy merchants, they contain 17th-century panelling, fireplaces and plaster ceilings. History includes the 18th-century love story of Bessie Surtees, who eloped from here in 1772 with John Scott, who became Lord Chancellor of England.

From the **Swing Bridge** (1876), which revolves through 90 degrees to allow ships to pass on either side, downstream to the new **Gateshead Millennium Bridge**, both banks of the Tyne have become the epicentre of Newcastle-Gateshead with a wealth of recent developments. The **Tyne Bridge**, symbol of the city, was completed in 1928 and looks beautiful at night. It took 80 years for it to be upstaged by the Gateshead Millennium Bridge half a mile upstream. The world's only tilting bridge, designed to look like a blinking eye, it too is impressively lit at night throwing patterns across the river. The footbridge leads over the river to the massive contemporary visual art space in the converted Baltic Flour Mill. The **BALTIC Centre for Contemporary Art** ① *South Shore Rd, Gateshead, T0191-478 1810, www.balticmill.com, Wed-Mon 1000-1800, Tue 1030-1800, free*, houses temporary exhibitions and provides studio space for artists. Definitely worth a look with its restaurants, cafés, bar, bookshop, and library, it's the north's answer to Tate Modern in London, although without the permanent collection of modern art.

Also on the Gateshead side of the river, across Baltic Square, Sir Norman Foster's glassy facility for all kinds of live music, **The Sage Gateshead** ① *St Mary's Sq, T0191-443 4661, www.thesagegateshead.org*, is a major regional centre for music-making of all kinds, from world-renowned classical and jazz artists to indie and folk, with an auditorium seating 1670. There's also a café, restaurant and four bars, all with great views over the Tyne.

Back on the Newcastle bank, the **Quayside** is home to the exciting **Live Theatre** (see entertainment, page 69) as well as a glinting array of restaurants and bars. A walk up into town from beneath the Tyne Bridge heads up busy Side and Dean streets into Grey Street, a remarkably unspoiled curving Victorian greystone street that leads up to the historic heart of Newcastle, **Grainger Town**. The area, including the Grainger Market (home to the original Marks & Spencer's Penny Bazaar), contains the city's finest Georgian and Victorian buildings, nearly half of which are listed. The focal point of Grainger Town is **Grey's Monument** which was erected when Earl Grey was prime minister, in honour of the Reform Act of 1832. Take a tour to the top of the monument for outstanding views across the city. From around the same era is the **Theatre Royal** ① *Grey St, T0844-811 2121, www.theatre-royal-newcastle.co.uk*, which underwent major refurbishment in 2011. With its lovely Victorian auditorium by Frank Matcham, it's the place to see touring opera, ballet, theatre and various spectacles for the family. There's a restaurant, tours, poetry and discussions and tearoom.

A short walk down New Bridge Street, the **Laing Art Gallery** ① *Higham Pl, T0191-232 7734, Mon-Sat 1000-1700, Sun 1400-1700, free*, is the grand Victorian repository of the city's art collection, including the 'Art on Tyneside' permanent collection, silver, glass and costume collections and the Proctor and Gamble Children's Gallery.

A good 15-minute walk further north, the **Great North Museum: Hancock** ① *Barras Bridge (Metro: Haymarket), T0191-222 6765, www.twmuseums.org.uk/great-north-museum, Mon-Sat 1000-1700, Sun 1300-1700, free*, opened its doors in 2009 as the result of a £26 million development project to incorporate the collections of Newcastle University's Shefton Museum of Antiquities, Greek Museum and former Hancock Museum. With displays on 'The Living Planet' and 'The Land of the Pharaohs', there's also a large-scale, interactive model of Hadrian's Wall, treasures from Ancient Greece, a planetarium, a virtual aquarium and a life-sized T-Rex skeleton replica. It's all very hands-on with plenty of touch-screen displays and interactive features.

Beaches around Newcastle

Just a short hop by Metro from the city are some lovely Blue Flag beaches. Perhaps the nicest stretch of sand is Longsands Beach at **Tynemouth**, a traditional seaside village with a 12th-century priory and castle. Despite the North Sea, there's a thriving surfing scene for the hardy, as well as a vibrant weekend market, lively pubs and a quirky market at weekends. A walk along the beach brings you to the **Blue Reef Aquarium** ① *Grand Parade, T0191-258 1031, www.bluereefaquarium.co.uk/tynemouth*, which has sharks, seals and otters amongst other things.

Just up the coast, the Victorian seaside town of **Whitley Bay** stretches from St Mary's Island in the north to Cullercoats in the south. Once a rival to Blackpool, complete with pleasure beach and fairground, the town is getting a much needed face-lift and once more promoting itself as a popular seaside destination. **St Mary's Lighthouse** ① *St Mary's Island, T0191-200 8652, stmaryslighthouse@northtyneside.gov.uk, £1.50*, is reached on foot by a causeway at low tide and can be climbed for good views of the coast.

On the south shores of the Tyne, a short hop on the ferry, **South Shields** has plenty of family attractions, including the Ocean Beach Pleasure Park and South Marine Park and an invigorating clifftop walk along The Leas to **Souter Lighthouse**. The excavated remains of **Arbeia Roman Fort** ① *Baring St, T0191-456 1369, www.twmuseums.org.uk/arbeia, Apr-Oct Mon-Fri 1000-1700, Sat 1100-1600, Sun 1400-1700*, dating back to AD 160, once guarded the River Tyne and has some impressive reconstructions to explore.

Hadrian's Wall listings

For hotel and restaurant price codes, and other relevant information, see pages 9-12.

⊜ Where to stay

Carlisle *p55*

££ Angus Hotel, 14-16 Scotland Rd, T01228-523546, www.angus-hotel.co.uk. 13 comfortable and quiet rooms with en suite bathrooms on the edge of the town over the river.

££ Langleigh House, 6 Howard Place, T01228-530440, www.langleighhouse.co.uk. Comfortable and roomy B&B in a pleasant part of town.

££ Number Thirty One, 31 Howard Place, T01228-597080, www.number31.co.uk. 4 rooms in an elegant and tastefully decorated Victorian townhouse in the middle of the town. Book well ahead.

£ Carlisle YHA, Old Brewery Residences, Bridge Lane, Caldewgate, T0845-371 9510. Jul-Sep only. A university hall of residence offering single rooms in flats for up to 7 people during university summer holidays.

East along Hadrian's Wall *p56*
A number of gastropubs also offer decent accommodation, see Restaurants, below.

££££ Farlam Hall, near Brampton, T01697-746234, www.farlamhall.co.uk. A Victorian country house hotel with amazing terraced gardens and very good walks round about.

££££-£££ Warwick Hall, Warwick-on- Eden, T01228-561546, www.warwickhall.org. Classic country house hotel, 2 miles from Carlisle. Luxury self-catering suites or stylish bedrooms. Fishing, clay pigeon shooting, tennis and golf on site.

£££ Beaumont Hotel, Beaumont St, Hexham, T01434-602331. Right in the middle of town and close to the abbey, with 34 comfortable en suite guest rooms.

£££-££ Sirelands, Heads Nook, Brampton, T01228-670389. Rural B&B with lovely gardens and a relaxed homely feel. Meals provided using home-grown vegetables.

££ Broomshaw Hill Farm, a mile outside Haltwhistle, T01434-321775, www.broom shaw.co.uk. Attractive 18th-century farmhouse B&B set in grassy woodland near the wall. Offers bicycle storage and will dry clothes/boots after muddy walks.

££ West Close House, Hextol Terrace, Hexham, T01434-603307, www.smoothound.co.uk/hotels/westclose. A fairly central 1920s guesthouse off Allendale Rd in a quiet cul-de-sac, a 10-min walk east of the abbey.

££-£ Greenhead Hotel and Hostel, Greenhead, near Brampton, T01697-747411, www.greenheadhotelandhostel.co.uk. From self-catering dorm rooms to comfortable en suite doubles, in a converted Methodist chapel close to Hadrian's Wall.

£ Ninebanks YHA, Orchard House, Mohope, Ninebanks, Hexham, T01434- 345288, www.ninebanks.org.uk. Recently renovated 17th-century cottage in a great location for exploring the local countryside.

£ Once Brewed YHA, Military Rd, Bardon Mill, T0845-371 9753, www.yha.org.uk/ hostel/once-brewed. With 90 beds mainly in 4-bedded rooms, a stone's throw from Vindolanda.

Camping

Hadrian's Wall Campsite, Melkridge Tilery, near Haltwhistle, T01434-320495, www.romanwallcamping.co.uk.

Newcastle and Gateshead *p58, map p60*
Newcastle has the full range of boutique hotels, chain hotels and apartments and B&Bs, along with some excellent youth hostels. Luxury business hotels include **The Hilton Newcastle Gateshead**,

Hotel Indigo Newcastle, Jury's Inn Newcastle and Jury's Inn Newcastle Gateshead Quays.

£££ Hotel du Vin, Allan House, City Rd, T0844-736 4259, www.hotelduvin.com. On the banks of the Tyne with fabulous views over the Quayside, 42 very comfortable rooms in a historic building. Excellent bar and wine cellar, as you might expect. Bistro-style restaurant offers classical brasserie menu overlooking the river with al fresco courtyard.

£££ Malmaison, 104 Quayside, T0191-245 5000, www.malmaison.com. Some weekend special offers. Creamy natural walls, crisp white sheets, rich royal spreads and throws. Chicly developed from a former co-op warehouse with modern rooms. French restaurant with view onto river. Eggs benedict, wild mushrooms polenta, thyme roasted sea bass are on offer in the restaurant.

£££ Townhouse Hotel, 1 West Av, Gosforth, T0191-285 6812, www.thetownhousehotel. co.uk. Boutique hotel in the leafy suburb of Gosforth. 10 individually designed luxury rooms with limestone wetrooms, Wi-Fi, plasma TV and thick piled carpets as standard. Lovely café attached.

£££-££ Jesmond Dene House Hotel, Jesmond Dene Rd, T0191-212 3000, www.jesmonddenehouse.co.uk. In a quiet woodland setting in the upmarket studenty suburb of Jesmond, 1 mile north of the centre. 40 contemporary rooms in an Arts and Crafts building with award-winning restaurant.

£££-££ Royal Station Hotel, Neville St, T0191-232 0781, www.royalstationhotel.com. A massive but beautiful grade I Victorian building right beside the station. All the rooms are spacious and comfortable, from family suites to executive doubles. The **Jalou Bar** is a bit trendy with peachy walls and wooden floors designed to create a Parisian ambience.

£££-££ Stables Lodge, South Farm, Lamesley, Gateshead, T0191-492 1756, www.thestableslodge.co.uk. On the southern edge of the city, close to the Angel of the North, this luxury B&B offers characterful 5-star accommodation in a semi rural setting.

££ Sleeperz Hotel, 15 Westgate Rd, T0191-261 6171, http://sleeperz.com/newcastle. Compact, cost-effective accommodation in the centre of town, close to the train station. All rooms have flatscreen TV and Wi-Fi.

£ Albatross Backpackers, 51 Grainger St, T0191-233 1330, www.albatrossnewcastle. co.uk. In the heart of historic Newcastle, the building retains some original features. Rooms from 2-12 people and all the usual facilities.

£ Euro Hostel, Carliol Sq, 10-min walk from Central Station, T08454-900371, www.euro-hostels.co.uk/newcastle. Good-value clean city centre hostel with range of rooms, breakfast and free Wi-Fi included.

£ Newcastle University Student Halls of Residence, T0191-2226296. Offers student rooms in the summer vacation, as does the **University of Northumbria**, T0191-2274204.

Beaches around Newcastle *p63*
Just a 30-min metro ride from the city centre, staying at the coast allows you to blow off the cobwebs after a hard day's sightseeing.

£££-££ Park Lodge, 158-160 Park Av, Whitley Bay, T0191-253 0288, www.park lodgewhitleybay.com. Family-run guesthouse near the beach offering comfortable rooms and a friendly welcome.

££ No 61 Guest House & Tea Rooms, 61 Front St, Tynemouth, T0191-257 3687, www.no61.co.uk. 100 m from Tynemouth castle. Smart, clean and characterful en suite rooms all recently renovated. Cosy tea room attached, with garden.

££ York House, 106-110 Park Av, Whitley Bay, www.yorkhousehotel.com. 14 en suite rooms, on site car parking, family-friendly.

Carlisle *p55*

££ David's, 62 Warwick Rd, T01228-523578, www.davidsrestaurant.co.uk. Long-standing elegant restaurant in a historic townhouse in the centre. Carlisle's finest dining experience.

££ Le Gall, 7 Devonshire St, T01228-818388. Atmospheric bistro with an eclectic menu of international dishes.

££-£ Alexandros, 68 Warwick Rd, T01228-592227, www.thegreek.co.uk. Family-run Greek restaurant serving generous mezze platters, as well as specials such as grilled octopus or seared chicken. Occasional live music.

£ Prior's Kitchen Restaurant, Paternoster Row Town Centre, T01228-543251, www.carlislecathedral.org.uk/priors_kitchen. Tea room housed in the former monks' dining room, beside the cathedral. Good for sandwiches, jacket potatoes and afternoon tea.

East along Hadrian's Wall *p56*

£££-££ Rat Inn, Alnwick, T01434-602814, www.theratinn.com. Traditional pub with good views out over the Tyne Valley. Daily specials board features hearty pub classics and some more ambitious dishes. Popular terraced beer garden in summer. Recommended.

££ The Barrasford Arms, Barrasford, T01434-681237, www.barrasfordarms.co.uk. Close to Kielder Water and Hadrian's Wall. Traditional 19th-century country inn serving classic British food with French influences, such as braised beef rump in Newcastle Brown Ale. Homely atmosphere. Also offers accommodation.

££ Duke of Wellington, Newton, T01661-844446, www.thedukeofwellingtoninn.co.uk. In a building dating from the 1600s, recently refurbished as a smart modern pub offering traditional British fine dining and real ales. Also offers accommodation.

££-£ Centre of Britain, Main St, Haltwhistle, T01434-322422, www.centre-of-britain.org.uk. Scandinavian-inspired decor and traditional menu that includes honey chilli duck breast or baked halibut with asparagus and prawn sauce. Large breakfasts to set you up for the day.

££-£ Milecastle, Military Rd, near Haltwhistle, T01434-321372, www.milecastle-inn.co.uk. An isolated and welcoming real ale pub with very decent pub grub, both at the bar, and in more sophisticated style in the restaurant.

£ Wallace Arms, Rowfoot, south of Haltwhistle off the A69 towards Alston, T01434-321872. A lovely old pub with excellent food and fine real ales.

Newcastle and Gateshead *p58, map p60*
Newcastle is blessed with a wide variety of very decent places to eat out. It's no surprise that the Quayside comes out top of the pops.

£££ Blackfriars Restaurant and Banquet Hall, Friars St, T0191 261 5945, www.blackfriarsrestaurant.co.uk. In a 13th-century Dominican friary, with split-level beamed dining area. Relaxed medieval feel with gutsy traditional dishes, winner of the Taste of England Award in the North East England Tourism Awards 2013.

£££ Café 21, Trinity Gardens, Quayside, T0191-222 0755, www.cafetwentyone.co.uk. Stylish open-plan brasserie, generally regarded as one of the best restaurants in the city with its bistro-style fusion menu with French undertones.

£££ Fisherman's Lodge, Jesmond Dene, T0191-281 3281, www.fishermanslodge.co.uk. In Heaton Park, a lakeside setting and wooded seclusion as well as serious cuisine make this one of the city's grandest dining experiences.

£££ Pan Haggerty, 21 Queen St, T0191-221 0904, www.panhaggerty.com. Stylish restaurant on the Quayside with a menu focussing on regional and British food.

£££ Six, BALTIC Centre for Contemporary Art, Gateshead Quays, T0191-440 4948, www.sixbaltic.com. Modern British brasserie with floor-to-ceiling windows affording a panoramic view over the Quayside.

£££-££ David Kennedy's Food Social, The Biscuit Factory, 16 Stoddart St, Sheildfield, T0191-260 5411, www.foodsocial.co.uk. Set in a former biscuit factory and now a commercial art gallery, this light and airy contemporary restaurant offers innovative brasserie dishes and tasty mature steaks.

£££-££ Jesmond Dene House, see Where to stay, above. One of Newcastle's finest dining experiences using fresh produce from the hotel garden and organic local ingredients such as Northumberland beef to create a traditional dishes with a twist.

££ Caffé Vivo, 29 Broad Chare, T0191-232 1331, www.caffevivo.co.uk. An Italian favourite, in a Quayside warehouse with a theatre attached. Uses authentic ingredients imported from Italy. Next door, its sister restaurant, **Broad Chare**, claims itself to be a 'proper pub' offering 'proper beer' and 'proper food', including hearty daily specials and Geordie-style tapas.

££ Electric East, St James Blvd, Waterloo Sq, T0191-221 1000, www.electric-east.co.uk. Innovative dishes from Cambodia, Thailand and Vietnam (including the 'shaking beef' special). Vibrant decor with Vietnamese artwork and lanterns.

££ Rasa, 27 Queen St, T0191-232 7799. On the Quayside, overlooking the Tyne. **Rasa**'s first restaurant outside London, serving authentic Keralan dishes, extensive menu. Good-value set lunch option.

££ Valley Junction 397, The Old Station, Archbold Terr, Jesmond, T0191-281 6397. An unusual and exceptional curry house in a converted junction box and railway carriage.

£ Olive & Bean, 17/19 Clayton St, T0191- 233 0990, www.oliveandbean.co.uk. Great coffee, smoothies and deli-style grub to eat in or take away.

Pubs, bars and clubs

Newcastle *p58, map p60*
Drinking is an activity that Newcastle takes seriously, and there are any number of different places to enjoy it. The main concentration of pubs, nightclubs and bars is around the Quayside and the Bigg Market, where crowds of locals flock to the bustling cobbled streets. Other popular areas include Collingwood St, Neville St, Osbourne St and around the Central Station. A fairly recent addition is 'The Gate' entertainment complex, which has a 12-screen multiplex cinema as well as numerous upmarket clubs and bars. The websites www.newcastlebynight.co.uk and www.pusbnewcastle.co.uk have further recommendations for a good night out on the 'toon'.

Pubs and bars
The Bacchus, 42-48 High Bridge, T0191- 261 1008. Close to the Theatre Royal, this traditional pub is covered in black and white images that reflect Tyneside's ship building past. Wide selection of cask ales and microbrewery beers.

The Centurion, Central Station, Neville St, T0191-261 6611, www.centurion-newcastle. com. Enjoy a drink in the splendour that was once the station's 1st-class waiting room (amazing Victorian tiling and murals).

The Cluny Warehouse, 36 Lime St, Ouseburn Valley, T0191-230 4474. A 15-min walk from the centre, a huge converted warehouse that's become a live-music venue and riverside art gallery of some note.

The Crown Posada, 31 The Side, T0191- 2321269. One of the oldest pubs in town. An unreconstructed boozer with Victorian stained-glass windows, also in the shadow of the Tyne Bridge.

Cumberland Arms, James Place St, T0191- 265 6151, www.thecumberlandarms.co.uk. Quirky pub in the Ouseburn Valley offering real ale and cider, live music and comedy. In winter there's an open fire, in summer a beer garden. Also has B&B rooms.

Living Room, Grey Street Hotel, 12 Grey St, T0191-255 4450, www.thelivingroom.co.uk. Piano bar and restaurant with a cool contemporary feel. Cocktails and live music.

The Pitcher and Piano, 108 Quayside, T0191-232 4110. In a prime position on the waterfront, with huge windows overlooking the Tyne and Gateshead Millennium Bridge. There's a vibrant mix at the bar.

Clubs

The Cut, 7 St Nicholas St, T0191-261 8579, www.whatisthecut.com. A derelict office building turned into a space for art projects and leftfield music club nights.

Digital, Times Sq, T0191-261 9755, www.yourfutureisdigital.com/newcastle. Newcastle's largest club attracting top DJs from around the world. Nights such as Turbulence have established it as the best drum 'n' bass night in the Northeast, while L.O.V.E on a Sat is also popular.

O2 Academy, Westgate Rd, T0191-260 2020, www.o2academynewcastle.co.uk. Large club that hosts some big names that get the whole place singing, chanting and raving.

Perdu Bar, 20 Collingwood St, T0191-2603040, www.perdubar.com. Late-night party venue with live music, DJs and cocktails with an outdoor lounge and secret garden.

Revolution, Collingwood St, T0191-261 6998, www.revolution-bars.co.uk/newcastleut. In a bank conversion with 30-ft ceilings and marble pillars, this bar is close to the Bigg Market and a massive hit with locals at weekends.

Riverside, 1 The Close, Quayside, T0191-230 1813, www.riversidenewcastle.co.uk. 2 floors of music catering to 1500 people a week (house, electro, dub, drum 'n' base) it's a popular choice with locals. The Voodoo Project on a Sat is always packed.

Tiger Tiger, The Gate, Newgate St, T0191-235 7065, www.tigertiger.co.uk. Large 3-floor club with various themed rooms. Try your

luck on the White Room dance floor, get into the retro party of Groovy Wonderland or sing your heart out in the Lucky Voice.

World Headquarters, Curtis Mayfield House, Carliol Sq, T0191-281 3445, www.welovewhq.com. Tucked away this 2-floor club is more intimate than some, with guest DJ nights attracting the likes of Zane Lowe. Popular with students, the dancefloor is always rammed and it gets pretty lively and sweaty.

⊕ Entertainment

Newcastle *p58, map p60*

Cinema

Side Cinema, 1-3 Side, T0191-232 2208, www.amber-online.com/sections/side-cinema. Small cinema run by a film and photography collective, showing art and independent films.

Star and Shadow, Stepney Bank, T0191-261 0066, www.starandshadow.org.uk. Showcases live art, films, gigs and exhibitions, anything that is 'new, different, underground, original'.

Tyneside Cinema, 10 Pilgrim St, T0845-217 9909, www.tynesidecinema.co.uk. For the film buff, showcase for London Film Festival tours.

Comedy

The **Metro Arena** and **City Hall** also attract big names in live comedy.

Hyena Comedy Club, 12 Leazes Lane, T0191-232 6030, www.thehyena.com.

The Stand Comedy Club, 31 High Bridge, T0844-693 3336, www.thestand.co.uk.

Live music

The Cluny Warehouse, Lime St, near Byker Bridge, T0191-230 4474. Good beer, staff and great for alternative music. Monthly jazz from big jazz stars and plenty of gigs from up-and-coming local bands.

Metro Radio Arena, Arena Way, T0844-493 6666, www.metroradioarena.co.uk. The largest concert and exhibition venue in the Northeast, attracting all the big names.

Newcastle Opera House, Westgate Rd, T0191-232 0899, www. newcastle operahouse.org. Capacity of 1100. Live mainstream rock, folk, pop and jazz venue.
The Sage Gateshead, St Mary's Sq, Gateshead Quays, T0191-443 4666, http://thesagegateshead.org. Provides top-class entertainment day and night with everything from intimate folk performances to large-scale symphonic extravaganzas.

Theatre

Live Theatre, 27 Broad Chare, Quayside, T0191-2321232, www.live.org.uk. Small city centre venue for new plays, music, dance and new writing, often with touring productions by national companies.
Northern Stage, Barras Bridge, T0191-230 5151, www.northernstage.co.uk. Middle-scale innovative classic and contemporary drama, considered one of the UK's top producing theatres.
Playhouse Whitley Bay, Marine Av, Whitley Bay, T0844-248 1588, www.playhousewhitley bay.co.uk. Opened in 2009, the £8.5 million refurbished venue hosts local and artistic drama groups as well as some big-name productions.
Theatre Royal, Grey St, T0870-9055060. Plays host to major touring companies like the RSC and National Theatre as well as ballet, opera and dance.

What to do

Newcastle *p58, map p60*
Football
Newcastle United Football Tour, Sports Direct Arena, Strawberry Place, T0191-261 1571, www.nufc.co.uk. More commonly known by its former name, St James Park, the home of Newcastle United towers over the city and has an atmosphere second to none. If you can't make a game, join a behind-the-scenes tour, £10, £7 children.

Sightseeing tours
City Sightseeing, www.citysightseeing-newcastlegateshead.com. Hop-on, hop-off bus that runs all across the city and stops at all the main sights. Tickets cost £8, £4 children and allow unlimited travel for a 24-hr period.

Transport

Newcastle *p58, map p60*
Bus
Long distance National Express, T08705-808080, www.nationalexpress.co.uk, serves Newcastle from most major UK cities, including: **Manchester** (5 hrs), **York** (2½ hrs), **London** (6 hrs 40 mins), **Durham** (30 mins), **Leeds** (2½ hrs) and **Edinburgh** (3 hrs).

Taxi
ABC Taxis, 1-3 Cross St, T0191-2323636; **Central Taxis**, Prudhoe St, Haymarket, T0191-2716363; **Noda Taxis**, Central Station, Neville St, T0191-2221888.

Train
GNER serve Newcastle from **London King's Cross** frequently throughout the day (3½ hrs). There are also direct services from **Birmingham** (3 hrs 45 mins), **Leeds** (1 hr 20 mins), **York** (1 hr), **Edinburgh** (1 hr 40 mins) and **Durham** (10 mins). For services from **Liverpool** and **Manchester**, change at Leeds.

Directory

Newcastle *p58, map p60*
Post office St Marys Place, T0845-722 3344. **C.L.E.O**, 23 Newbiggin Hall Centre, T0191-286 2694. **Hospitals The Royal Victoria Infirmary**, Queen Victoria Rd, T0191-232 5131. **Police** Newcastle City Centre Police Station, Market St, T0191-214 6555.

County Durham

Until relatively recently, County Durham was synonymous with mining: limestone and lead in the west and coal on the coast. Most of the coal pits were closed down in the 1970s and early 1980s, often with terrible consequences for the local communities. Some have recovered since, especially along the coast, which has been given a thorough clean-up. The western part of the county stretches into the Pennines towards Cumbria, and the valleys of the Wear and the Tees lure in hillwalkers and ramblers. Barnard Castle is the market town at the heart of the area, with the magnificent ruined fortification and an interesting stately home at Bowes, its main attractions. The highlight of a visit to the county, however, is still Durham itself, dominated by what is arguably the most impressive Romanesque cathedral in Europe. Described by Bill Bryson as 'a perfect little city', it has a handful of interesting museums, galleries, boutiques and cafés, but once you've seen the cathedral, you've pretty much seen it all.

Durham → *For listings, see pages 77-79.*

Durham presents passing train travellers with a wonderful spectacle: stacked up half a mile away on a ridge in a tight loop of the River Wear, its massive cathedral towers up behind the castle, a grey-brown stone fantasy of a place. Visually it's unlikely to disappoint day-trippers either, although there's not a huge amount more to do than wander over the river on to the 'peninsula' and up to the cathedral, enjoying the compact and cobbled centre of this university town. After the cathedral, a tour of the castle might come as a bit of a disappointment, though there are a couple of decent museums, including the university-owned Museum of Archaeology and the unusual Oriental Museum, a mile to the south on the main campus. The opening of the Gala centre in Millennium Place beside Millburngate Bridge has brought new life to the city with a state-of-the-art visitor centre, theatre, cinema, library and café complex. Otherwise Durham makes a reasonable base from which to explore the hillwalking delights of Weardale and Teesdale in the Pennine hills to the west.

Arriving in Durham

Getting there GNER run about 17 express west coast **trains** to Durham from London King's Cross daily, taking about 2½-three hours. Durham is just off the A1 (M) linking it to north and south, about 260 miles from London, a journey that usually takes about 5 hours. From the west, the A68 'holiday route' crosses Northumberland and Border Country. **National Express**, T08705-808080, service 425 runs five times a day to Durham from London Victoria, including a nightbus, leaving at 0830, 1230, 1500, 1730 and 2330. The journey takes just over 6 hours. Durham is also connected by coach to Newcastle and York. ▶▶ *See Transport, page 79.*

Getting around The medieval centre of Durham can easily be negotiated on foot. All the main sights are located within half a square mile on the peninsula of the river Wear. In fact, Durham pioneered congestion charging in Britain with its £2 charge for cars using the town centre from Monday to Saturday 1000-1600. The paypoint is next to St Nicholas' church at the entrance to the market place. Durham Cathedral Bus no 40 runs from the Coach Park and train station to the cathedral via the Market Place, every 20 minutes Monday to Friday 0805-1725, Saturday 0905-1725, Sunday 0945-1645. Local buses run out to the university campus and Durham Art Gallery. **Traveline**, T0870-6082608.

Tourist information There's no tourist information centre as such, but **This is Durham** ① *T03000-262626, www.thisissdurham.com, Mon-Sat 0930-1730, Sun 1100-1600*, provides a helpful telephone and online information service.

Background

A Saxon monastery was founded where Durham Cathedral now stands in 998. It was built around the church containing the body of St Cuthbert brought here three years earlier. He actually died in 687 but the miraculously preserved corpse of this father of the Celtic Church had been carried around the north for more than a century by monks from his monastery at Lindisfarne, fleeing Danish raiders in the ninth century. Apparently they found the sacred spot by following a dun cow. (The grey-brown ruminant is commemorated by a carving near the cathedral's east end and Dun Cow Lane.) A few years after the Conquest, the Norman emissary to Durham was slaughtered on arrival. When the Normans came back, their revenge was brutal, William himself overseeing the 'Harrying of the North', only complete in 1075. Walcher of Lorraine replaced the monastery with a Benedictine institution with monks borrowed from Monkwearmouth on the coast. Work started on the cathedral that stands today in 1093 and was all but complete – barring the towers – by 1140. Its first bishop, William of St Calais, introduced the French style in its architecture. He

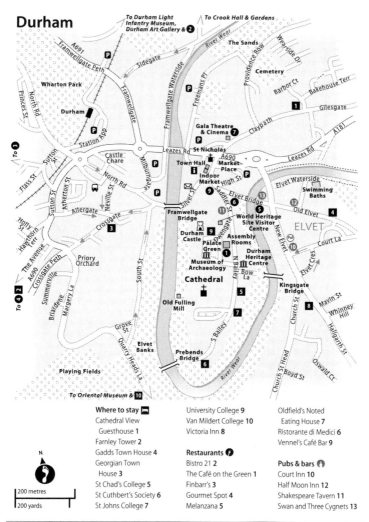

Durham

Where to stay 🛏	University College 9	Oldfield's Noted
Cathedral View	Van Mildert College 10	Eating House 7
Guesthouse 1	Victoria Inn 8	Ristorante di Medici 6
Farnley Tower 2		Vennel's Café Bar 9
Gadds Town House 4	**Restaurants** 🍴	
Georgian Town	Bistro 21 2	**Pubs & bars** 🍺
House 3	The Café on the Green 1	Court Inn 10
St Chad's College 5	Finbarr's 3	Half Moon Inn 12
St Cuthbert's Society 6	Gourmet Spot 4	Shakespeare Tavern 11
St Johns College 7	Melanzana 5	Swan and Three Cygnets 13

N

200 metres
200 yards

was the first of the so-called Prince Bishops, clerics with almost as many powers as the King, who ruled this virtual buffer-state between England and Scotland until the modern period. In the 19th century, Durham County became famous for its surrounding coal fields until the closure of most pits in the late 20th century.

Places in Durham

After taking a minute to enjoy the view from the train station, on high ground in the west of the city, it's a 15-minute walk downhill over the river to the centre. The most direct route is also the best, heading down North Road past the bus station to pedestrianized Framwelgate Bridge. From here there are more fine views of the castle walls up above, before the steep climb up to the **Market Place** via Silver Street. As well as the grand Town Hall and Victorian covered market, the Market Place boasts a fine statue of Neptune, God of the Sea. The spire of **St Nicholas Church** at the entrance to Market Place is a useful landmark.

A right turn from here leads up Saddler Street towards the heart of the peninsula. Down to the left, Elvet Bridge slopes off across the river again to the Elvet district, the city's administrative centre with its classiest hotels, **The Royal** and the **Three Tuns**. Cobbled Owengate on the right again climbs the short distance up to Palace Green, the wide open lawn dividing cathedral and castle at the top of the hill.

Cathedral

ⓘ *T0191-3864266, www.durhamcathedral.co.uk, Mon-Sat 0730-1800, Sun 0745-1730; Jul-Sep open until 2000, entry by donation. Tower: Apr-Sep Mon-Sat 1000-1600 (last entry 1540), Oct-Mar Mon-Sat 1000-1500 (last entry 1440), Sun 1300-1430, £5, children £2.50. Guided tours: Apr-Oct Mon-Sat 1030, 1100, 1400, £5, children free.*

Durham Cathedral is the most superb Norman survival in England, a fact recognized by its designation as a World Heritage Site, but its striking position, remarkable state of preservation and sheer size are what make first impressions so immediately rewarding. A powerful statement of the authority of the Norman Conquest, this is still a place with presence. On the north door, the main entrance, hangs a replica (the original is in the Treasures of St Cuthbert Museum in the cloisters) of the Sanctuary Knocker, used by criminals and exiles seeking safe haven and passage to the coast.

Once inside, the eye is drawn down the long nave toward the round east window by the huge columns supporting the vault of the nave: this was the first church in Europe to be rib-vaulted throughout, its piers alternately rounded or clustered, the round ones decorated with geometric patterns. Approaching the high altar they spiral up towards heaven. Highlights of the interior, apart from the overall impression, include the **Galilee Chapel** at the west end, which contains the tomb of the Venerable Bede, (his *Ecclesiastical History of the English People*, written in the eighth century, long set the benchmark for early histories of the country); the tombs of the powerful **Neville family**; **Prior Castell's Clock**, an early-16th-century clock restored in 1938; the **Bishops Throne** in the choir, that of Prince Bishop Hatfield (1345-1381); the **Miners Memorial** in the nave; and beyond the Frosterley Marble Bar, marking the limit of women's permitted access to the monastic church, the **shrine of St Cuthbert** himself in the Chapel of Nine Altars. The shrine was demolished during the Reformation, and the saint now lies buried beneath a marble slab. South of the main body of the cathedral, the original monastic buildings clustered around the cloisters, built in the early 15th century. The monk's dormitory with its fine timber roof can be seen, although more interesting perhaps are the **Treasures of St Cuthbert**, a revamped exhibition of the cathedral's valuables, including a piece of the saint's coffin and some of the relics found inside. Look out too for the original **Sanctuary Knocker** and some extraordinary illuminated manuscripts. Finally, the views from the top of the **tower** on a fine day are well worth the modest charge.

Castle

ⓘ *www.dur.ac.uk/event.durham/venues/colleges/durham.castle, daily 1000-1700; 40-min guided tours term-time at 1400, 1500 and 1600, also at 1000, 1100 and 1200 during university holidays, £5, children £3, family £12, contact T0191-334 2932 to arrange.*

Opposite the north side of the cathedral, a couple of hundred yards away across Palace Green, the castle was started in the early 1070s, a key element in William the Conqueror's subjugation of the north. Although the arch of the gateway is original, additions and renovations to the whole castle were undertaken in the 19th century when it became the first college of the university. Like Oxford and Cambridge, **Durham University** operates a collegiate system. Guided tours of the place include the Great Hall, with its 14th-century roof, the late 17th-century Black Staircase and the Norman chapel.

Other sights in the city

Between the cathedral and the castle, the **Museum of Archaeology** ⓘ *Wolfson Gallery, Palace Green, www.dur.ac.uk/museums, Apr-Oct daily 1100-1600, Nov-Mar Fri-Mon 1130-1530, £1, children 50p,* is in the process of moving from its former home in the Old Fulling Mill building to brand new premises in the Palace Green Library, due to open in 2014. Check the website for details. Owned by the university, the museum will provide illuminating hands-on activities and displays on the very early history of the area. The university's other museum, the **Oriental Museum** ⓘ *Elvet Hill, T0191-334 5694, www.dur.ac.uk/oriental.museum, Mon-Fri 1000-1700, Sat, Sun 1200-1700, £1.50, children free,* is based in the university campus to the south and contains a collection of ancient Egyptian, Chinese and Japanese sculptures and artworks. It's the only museum in northern England dedicated entirely to oriental art and antiquities.

A short hop from the cathedral, on the east side of the peninsula in the old church of St Mary-le-Bow overlooking little Kingsgate Bridge, the **Durham Heritage Centre** ⓘ *St Mary-Le-Bow, North Bailey, T0191-384 5589, www.durhamheritagecentre.org.uk, Jun-Sep daily 1100-1630, May and Oct weekends only 1400-1630,* is a local history museum with displays on the mining industry, crime and punishment and medieval Durham.

Heading north back through heart of the city, the **Gala Theatre and Cinema** ⓘ *Millennium Place, T0191-332 4041, www.galadurham.co.uk,* beside Millburngate Bridge, is a £1.5 million development and the centrepiece of Durham's art scene. On the banks of the Wear, the complex includes a state-of-the-art theatre, cinema, library and café-bar and provides an entertaining night out.

On the other side of the river, along Sidegate, are the **Crook Hall and Gardens** ⓘ *T0191-384 8028, www.crookhallgardens.co.uk,* a medieval hall set in 4 ha of gardens and visited by Wordsworth in the 1800s. Said to be haunted by the White Lady, the hall contains a Jacobean drawing room, turret and gallery, while the gardens include two beautiful walled gardens, an orchard, fountain, moat pool and maze. It's attractive in all seasons and there's a pleasant courtyard café.

Walks in County Durham

Cronkley Fell 7 miles there and back. Start: Forest-in-Teesdale, 15 miles west of Barnard Castle. A climb up into the lower regions of Mickle Fell in the Lune Forest to a wonderful nature reserve. OS Maps: *Outdoor Leisure 31*.

High Force 6 miles there and back. Start: Holwick, 12 miles west of Barnard Castle. A walk along part of the Pennine Way alongside the Tees to the famous waterfall High Force. OS Maps: *Outdoor Leisure 31*.

Hunderthwaite Moor 4 miles there and back. Start: Kelton, 10 miles west of Barnard Castle. A gentle stroll on to the moors overlooking the Selset and Balderhead Reservoirs. OS Maps: *Outdoor Leisure 31*.

Hamsterley Forest 3 mile circle. Start: Redford, 12 miles north of Barnard Castle. Forest walks and nature trails in a well-managed beauty spot. OS Maps: *Outdoor Leisure 31*.

Easington Colliery 4 miles there and back. Start: Easington Colliery. A breezy beach and low clifftop walk along the renovated east coast. OS Maps: *Explorer 308*.

In the northwest of the city, the **Durham Light Infantry Museum and Durham Art Gallery** ⓘ *Aykley Heads, T03000-266590, http://county.durham.gov.uk/sites/dli, Apr-Oct daily 1000-1700, Nov-Mar daily 1000-1600, £3.60, children £1.60*, is one of the North's finest military museum and traces the heroic history of the regiment from 1758-1968. There are opportunities for hands-on exploration with interactive displays, object handling and craft workshops. The art gallery hosts interesting temporary exhibitions as well as events such as concerts, talks and practical workshops.

County Durham, Weardale and Teesdale

Around Durham

Twelve miles northwest of Durham, **Beamish – The Living Museum of the North** ⓘ *Beamish, near Stanley, T0191-370 4000, www.beamish.org.uk, Mar-Oct daily 1000-1700, Nov-Feb Tue-Thu only, last admission 1500, £17.50, children (age 5-15) £10, tickets valid for 12 months*, is a living, working museum that allows you to experience what everday rural and urban life was like in the Northeast in the early 20th century. Set in 300 acres of countryside, costumed demonstrators bring to life the Edwardian Town and Pit Village, where you can test your handwriting skills on a slate before putting on a hard hat and venturing down into an original drift mine. At Home Farm and Pockerley Old Hall, you can witness how the industrial revolution transformed agriculture in the region or take a ride on a replica steam train. The buildings you see at Beamish have been carefully reconstructed from the originals to give visitors a real sense of history.

East of Durham the black coal mining coast that featured to memorable effect in the cult Michael Caine film *Get Carter* has been so thoroughly cleaned up that locals hardly recognize it. The beaches around Easington Colliery now make for refreshing breezy walks but the area round about remains rather depressed.

Weardale and Teesdale

West of the city, the A690/A689 runs through the Pennine Valley of the Wear, Weardale, to the Cumbrian market town of **Alston**. There aren't many sights as such en route, but the road passes through some impressively wild and remote scenery, popular with hillwalkers. Almost parallel with the valley of the Wear to the south, Teesdale is similar but more touristy. Visitors come here to walk, but there are also waterfalls like **High Force**, certainly true to its name when the river's in spate, which draw in the punters. **Barnard Castle** ① *(EH), T01833-638212, Apr-Sep daily 1000-1800, Oct-Mar weekends 1000-1600, £4.40, children £2.60*, is the heart of the area, a fairly attractive market town dominated by the ruined fortification beside the Tees. Once one of the largest in England, it was the principal seat of the powerful Baliol family, who often held the balance of power between England and Scotland. The romantic ruins overlook the river, surrounded by acres of gardens, including a 'sensory' one.

A mile or so east of Barnard Castle, on the edge of town, the **Bowes Museum** ① *T01833-690606, www.bowesmuseum.org.uk, daily 1100-1700. £9, children free*, is housed in a Victorian French chateau purpose-built to show off the fine art collection of industrialist John Bowes. Antique furniture and ceramics surround an important array of Old Masters, including two Canalettos.

Continuing east along the A688, the National Railway Museum at Shildon, **Locomotion** ① *T01388-77999, www.nrm.org.uk, Apr-Sep daily 1000-1700, Oct-Mar daily 1000-1600*, is a family-friendly attraction with over 70 vehicles including the first ever steam hauled passenger train which operated during the opening ceremony of the Stockton and Darlington Railway in 1825. Visitors can take a ride on a steam train and there are special events throughout the year.

County Durham listings

For hotel and restaurant price codes, and other relevant information, see pages 9-12.

● Where to stay

Durham *p71, map p72*

££££-£££ Gadds Town House, 34 Old Elvet, T0191-384 1037, www.gaddstownhouse.com. Set in an 18th-century Georgian townhouse, this boutique hotel in the centre of Durham offers 11 luxury rooms and a secluded garden apartment. Smart restaurant attached. Packages available.

£££ Farnley Tower, The Avenue, T0191-3750011, www.farnleytower.co.uk. There is indeed a tower, but that's not the main feature of this friendly upmarket B&B, which provides comfortable accommodation on the western edge of the city.

££ Cathedral View Guesthouse, Claypath, 212 Gilesgate, T0191-386 9566, www.cathedralview.com. True to its name from a couple of its rooms at least, this is a comfortable smart B&B close to Millennium Place in a former Georgian merchant's house dating from 1734.

££ The Georgian Town House, 10 Crossgate, T0191-386 8070, www.the georgiantownhousedurham.co.uk. Attractive grade II listed building about 5 mins' walk from the market place, some rooms with views of the cathedral. Attached is **The Pancake Café**.

££ Victoria Inn, 86 Hallgarth St, T0191-386 5269, www.victoriainn-durhamcity.co.uk. Family-run B&B in a grade II listed building a 5-min walk from the castle. 6 comfortable en suite rooms refurbished in 2012. Off-street parking, hearty breakfasts and Wi-Fi.

££-£ University of Durham Halls of Residence, T0800-289970, www.dur.ac.uk/event.durham/tourism. B&B accommodation in the university holidays from £32.50 per person. For location try the **University College**, Palace Green, in the castle itself, or **St Johns College**, 3 South Bailey, next to the cathedral, or **St Cuthbert's Society**, 12 South Bailey, on the river in the crux of the bend, and **St Chad's College**, 18 North Bailey. Just outside the city, on the main university campus, **Van Mildert College**, Mill Hill Lane, is more modern and marginally more comfortable with a good canteen.

County Durham, Weardale and Teesdale *p75*

£££ Rose and Crown, Barnard Castle, T01833-650213, www.rose-and-crown.co.uk. 18th-century coaching inn with 12 en suite rooms in the main house or courtyard. Some with beams and antique furniture others are more modern. All are comfortable and well-equipped. Good restaurant attached.

£££-££ Cooper House Farm, Cotherstone, Barnard Castle, T01833-650187, www.cooperhouse.org.uk. Upmarket farmhouse B&B set in beautiful countryside. Comfortable guest sitting room. Breakfast eggs provided by the resident chickens.

● Restaurants

Durham *p71, map p72*

Thanks to the student population, there's no shortage of places to eat a lot very cheaply in Durham. There are a scattering of upmarket options too.

£££-££ Finbarr's, Waddington St, Flass Vale, T0191-370 9999, www.finbarrsrestaurant. co.uk. Opened in 2010, **Finbarr's** is Durham's answer to a quality restaurant in a chic, contemporary setting, serving up dishes such as seared scallops with belly pork and artichoke purée or half lobster with garlic butter and hand cut chips. Good wine list,

£££-££ Gadds Townhouse, 34 Old Elvet, T0191-384 1037, www.gaddstown

house.com. A smart option in the centre of town. Starters include caviar, scallops or oysters, followed by monkfish, calves liver or fillet steak. Sandwiches and light bites available during the day.

£££-££ Gourmet Spot, The Avenue, T0191-384 6655, www.gourmet-spot.co.uk. Specializes in innovative cuisine and aims to source ingredients from within a 30-mile radius. 2-course à la carte menu for £32, market menu for £20 or a vegetarian tasting menu for £50. All accompanied by fine wines and a classy ambience.

££ Bistro 21, Aykley Heads House, Aykley Heads, T0191-384 4354. Probably the best mid-range option. It does good value English food in a cosy place, with set lunches for about £12, but it's some way from the centre, near the DLI Museum and Art Gallery.

££ Oldfields Noted Eating House, 18 Claypath, T0191-370 9595, http://oldfields eatinghouse.com. The former premises of the Durham Gas Company, dating back to 1881, have been converted into a light and airy dining space. Specializing in 'real British food, cooked properly', with treats such as pan haggerty (a northeast speciality), rabbit and black pudding casserole and beef and oyster cottage pie on the menu.

££ Vennel's Café Bar, Saddler St, behind Waterstone's bookshop, T0191-375 0623. Tucked away up a little alleyway, this popular and busy wholefood café offers the freshest scones in town as well as a selection of home-made bread and soup.

£ The Café on the Green, Palace Green, T0191-334 3688. Located in the 15th-century almshouse buildings between the castle and the cathedral, this café is a good spot for lunch with fresh home-made food.

£ Melanzana, 96 Elvet Bridge, T0191-384 0096, www.melanzanadurham.co.uk. Italian café bar-bistro set within the chapel of St Andrew's serving pizza, pasta and other Mediterranean fare.

£ Ristorante di Medici, 21 Elvet Bridge, T0191-3861310. Another Italian joint doing pizza or pasta deals, popular with students.

Pubs, bars and clubs

Durham *p71, map p72*
The Court Inn, Court Lane, Elvet, T0191-384 7350, www.courtinn.co.uk. Has a cult following with sporty students because of its filling grub.
Half Moon Inn, 86 New Elvet, T0191-374 1918, www.thehalfmooninndurham.co.uk. Traditional city centre pub serving cask ales.
Shakespeare Tavern, 66 Saddler St, T0191-384 3261. An unbeatably authentic traditional locals' pub with very good beer.
Swan and Three Cygnets, Elvet Bridge, T0191-384 0242. In a lovely location by the river, the beer garden is popular in summer.
Victoria Inn, 86 Hallgarth St, T0191-386 5269, www.victoriainn-durhamcity.co.uk. Friendly pub specializing in cask ales, with a fine selection of whisky. See Where to stay.

Entertainment

Durham *p71, map p72*
Gala Theatre, Millennium Place, T0191-332 4041, www.galadurham.co.uk. Durham's state-of-the-art cultural hub with regular touring theatre productions, comedians, musicians and a cinema.

Shopping

Durham *p71, map p72*
Durham Indoor Market has almost 100 different stalls in a Victorian building on Market Place, T0191-384 6153.
Farmer's markets every 3rd Thu of the month 0930-1530.
Mugwump, 37 Saddler St, stocks interesting gifts and costumes, one of a strip of shops on Elvet Bridge worth a browse.
Town Hall Craft Fairs every 4th Sat of the month, 0930-1630.

⚠ What to do

Durham *p71, map p72*
Bicycle
Specialist Cycles, within Meadowfield and District Soc, Frederick St South, Meadowfield, T0191-378 3753.

Boating
Prince Bishop River Cruise, Brown's Boathouse, Elvet Bridge, T0191-386 9525. £3.50, children £1.50. 1-hr cruises with views of the cathedral, castle and bridges. Commentary includes history, natural history and geography.

City tours
Durham Ghost Walk, T0191-384 6583, www.durhamghostwalk.co.uk. Walks take place on 1st Sun of the month at 2000 and leave from Durham Market Place under the horse statue, for an alternative history of the city.

⊖ Transport

Durham *p71, map p72*
Car
Enterprise Rent-a-Car Ltd, Enterprise Premises, Darlington Rd, Nevilles Cross, T0191-386 8666; **S Jennings**, High St, Carrville, T0191-384 6655.

Taxi
Direct Taxis, The Warehouse, Rennys Lane, T0191-3862002; **Pratts Taxis**, Maven House, Frankland La, T0191-386 0700.

❶ Directory

Durham *p71, map p72*
Medical services University Hospital, Lancaster Rd, T0191-333 2300. **Police** Durham Police HQ, Aykley Heads, T0191-386 4929. **Post office** 33 Silver St, T0845-722 3344.

Northumberland

North of Newcastle and embracing the best bits of Hadrian's Wall, the wilds of Northumberland are a remote haven for naturalists, historians and hikers. From Alnwick to Berwick, the coast plunges in and out of the North Sea around rocky headlands, ruined castles and windswept fishing villages. Offshore, the Farne Islands support an extraordinary variety of seabirds, while Holy Island provided sanctuary for the early Celtic Christian church in the seventh century. Alnwick itself was recently voted by *Country Life* readers the most desirable town in the UK in which to live, going some way towards explaining the popularity of green wellies, working dogs and conservative attitudes throughout the county. Its castle is still the ancestral home of the Duke of Northumberland, and the gardens have been given a multimillion-pound makeover by the Duchess. On the border with Scotland, Berwick-upon-Tweed has an embattled charm born of its deeply disputed history. Inland, much of the rest of the county is taken up with the Northumberland National Park, an ancient granite plug surrounded by mile upon mile of the kind of carboniferous limestone that forms the bedrock of Ireland. Recent campaigns by conservationists have encouraged the return of indigenous wild flowers and grasses across many parts of this beautiful moorland.

Alnwick and the coast → *For listings, see pages 88-91.*

Walking or driving along anywhere between Alnwick and Berwick is a rare pleasure: few cars, fewer walkers and miles of superb empty beaches, though swimming and sunbathing are perhaps only for the hardiest. The coast unfolds a landscape of spectacular beauty, dotted with the country's finest selection of castles and home to a wide variety of birds and wild flowers. The long swathes of sand are punctuated by rocky promontories and quiet fishing villages that are gradually turning into quiet resorts and retirement homes as the fish disappear and, though not picturesque, they get on with the job as unobtrusively as possible. Out to sea, the Farne Islands promise prolific birdlife while across the causeway on Holy Island lies the bleak outpost that produced the vigorous flower of early English Christianity.

Arriving in Alnwick and the coast
Getting there Intercity and local rail services run along the mainline Edinburgh to London route, fast trains calling four times a day at Alnmouth, about 5 miles from Alnwick itself, Berwick (30 minutes), Newcastle (40 minutes) and Edinburgh (40 minutes). Newcastle has frequent trains from London (four hours). **National Rail Enquiries**, T08457-484950. The A1 runs between Newcastle and Berwick while the scenic route hugs the coast more closely. Newcastle to Alnwick takes 45 minutes and Alnwick to Berwick the same again. To the southwest, the B3642 runs down to Rothbury, Hexham and the Wall and the B6346. **National Express** ① *T08705-808080, www.nationalexpress.co.uk*, service X18 runs between Newcastle and Berwick, making a stop at Alnwick, also calling at Warkworth and Alnmouth for connections to the train.

Getting around Arriva ① *T0191-212 3000, www.arrivabus.co.uk*, runs a good if infrequent network of local buses along the coast. Cycling is very popular locally, and there are cycle routes in abundance along the flattish coast.

Tourist information Alnwick TIC ① *The Shambles opposite the market place, T01665-511333, www.visitalnwick.org.uk, Mon-Sat 0900-1700, Sun 1000-1600*. The **Northumbria Tourist Board** website www.visitnortheastengland.com, has a wealth of tourist and orientation information. The website www.visitnorthumberland.com is also useful.

Alnwick
This charming town quite simply has it all: a magnificent castle, cobbled streets, a breezy local welcome, spectacular views over the Cheviot Hills and bright, clean air. Though small enough to easily find your way around, Alnwick (pronounced Annick) wears its rich historical grandeur with grace yet is far enough away to avoid overcrowding even in high season. Elizabeth I felt sufficiently uncomfortable about the wealth of the Dukes of Northumberland and their distant estates centred round Alnwick that for many years the earl was forbidden to visit his lands on pain of death. Stroll round the market place and take in the characteristically ambitious new gardens laid out for the millennium when the sun shines, or lose yourself in the castle's palatial interior and enjoy the fast, good natured banter in one of the town's many pubs when the sharp northeasterlies blow through and you cannot help but notice the strong, almost feudal sense of pride and independence.

Alnwick Castle ① T01665-510777, www.alnwickcastle.com, Apr-Oct daily 1100-1700 (last admission 1615), Nov-Apr daily 1000-1800, £14, children (5-16 years) £7, like its town, comes complete in medieval splendour with all the trimmings: imposing gatehouse, majestic lions and cobbled courtyards. It has been in the Percy family since 1309 and in active military use for the following 250 years, playing an important part in the incessant border wars. In the 18th century, the first duke – they had been humble earls until then – undertook the first of several rounds of restoration thereby making it into one of the grandest stately homes on the circuit. After Windsor it is the largest inhabited castle in the country and there is certainly a luxurious if not royal feeling of grandeur about the place. Lofty state rooms with Adam interiors are hung with paintings by Canaletto, Van Dyck and Titian, high windows overlook a Capability Brown landscape, elegant cabinets overflow with Meissen in the dining room while the library boasts one of the finest collections of books in the country. Watch out for Harry Potter fans on pilgrimage to locations used in the film.

Alnwick Garden ① Denwick Lane, T01665-511350, www.alnwickgarden.com, £12, children (5-16 years) £4, is an extraordinary contemporary garden masterminded by the current duchess. A monumental cascade takes centre stage, its fountains periodically erupting in great bursts while paths meander along the carefully planted beds in the walled garden above. The huge scale might initially seem stark but given time, the garden should grow into its own, delighting rather than overpowering the senses.

Book lovers and train enthusiasts will find rich pickings at **Barter Books** ① T01665-604888, www.barterbooks.co.uk, daily 0900-1900, housed in the former Alnwick Station. Starting off in what was the ticket and parcel office, the bookshop has expanded down the platforms and through the waiting rooms, until it now covers over one-quarter of the whole station site. Over 8000 sq ft, 350,000 books, 3 miles of shelving and a model train that runs round the lot. Cakes, tea and coffee are available for the sore of foot or eye.

A short walk from Barter Books, the **Bakehouse Gallery** ① Prudhoe St, T01665-602277, www.thebakehousegallery.com, showcases contemporary works of art, including felted sculptures, wall hangings and vintage silk, while the **Bailiffgate Museum and Gallery** ① 14 Bailiffgate, T01665-605847, www.bailiffgatemuseum.co.uk, Easter-Oct daily 1000-1600, Nov-Easter closed Tue, £2.50, children free, explores the history of Alnwick and the surrounding area with permanent and temporary art and history exhibitions and various hands-on activities.

The **Aln Valley Railway** ① www.alnvalleyrailway.co.uk, which runs 2.75 miles from Alnwick to Alnmouth, once part of the East Coast Main Line, is undergoing an ambitious restoration project with the aim of re-opening sometime in 2013. See website for details.

Alnmouth and Warkworth

The town's port at **Alnmouth** has a picturesque harbour which had a bustling trade with Norway, Holland and London during its heyday in the 18th century. Now it sits happily at the mouth of the River Aln welcoming holiday makers, walkers, hardy swimmers and cream tea enthusiasts with colourful warmth. A must for the die-hard bucket and spade brigade.

A 5-mile walk south along a beautiful stretch of sand will bring you to the small town of **Warkworth**, dominated by a particularly impressive **castle** ① (EH), T01665-711423, Apr-Sep daily 1000-1800, Oct 1000-1700, Nov-Mar 1000-1600 (closed 1300-1400), £4.90, children (5-15 years) £2.90, dating from the 14th century, proud on a hill above a bend in the River Coquet. Also owned by the Percy family, it's understandable that even they were unable to keep up two such establishments so close to each other. The unrestored ruins here, however, give a good idea of how a purely military castle gradually changed into a fortified house: note particularly the enormous fireplaces and spartan bed chambers. Its dramatic setting is put to good use in Shakespeare's *Henry IV*. It is also possible to visit **Warkworth Hermitage**, a mile up the river. Dating from the late 15th century, some say it was founded by a murderer atoning for the death of his brother, others by a warrior who was mourning the loss of his sweetheart. **Warkworth Church** also has a good interior despite its troubled early life: burnt to the ground by invading Scots as early as the 12th century, it was rebuilt and though it has a mixture of Norman, Gothic and Jacobean elements, they contribute to a pleasing whole.

The ruins of **Dunstanburgh Castle** ① *(EH), T01665-576231, Apr-Oct 1000-1800 daily, Nov-Mar 1000-1600 Wed-Sun, £4, children (5-15 years)£2.40,* built in the 14th century high above the waves on a rocky outcrop, are among the most evocative and romantically positioned of any in the country. Created by John of Gaunt, it was fortified during The Wars of the Roses only to fall into disuse thereafter. Although only the gatehouse and some of the walls remain, the 30-minute walk up to the castle from Craster and the longer stretches beyond along the Bays of Embleton and Beadnell are richly rewarding whatever the weather. In fact, dark clouds and rain suit Dunstanburgh as diamonds would the Ritz. Golfers can admire the castle from the greens of the nearby course.

Bamburgh

Bamburgh's village green, complete with church, pub, hotel, butcher and baker, is quintessentially English and its pedigree is impeccable. In Anglo-Saxon times, it was the royal capital of the Kingdom of Northumbria and looking up at the **castle** ① *T01668-214515, www.bamburghcastle.com, mid-Feb to Oct daily 1000-1700, Nov to mid-Feb weekends only 1100-1630, £9.75, children (5-15 years) £4.25,* its Norman keep still standing proud and its high walls crowning a magnificent natural fortress, you'll see why. The panoramic view from the top is knockout, sweeping in most of the coastline and a good deal of the beautiful country inland, though the chilly interior has little of interest except the comprehensive collection of Victorian kitchenware in its bare scullery. The village also comes with a towering Victorian heroine in the shape of Grace Darling, the brave daughter of a lighthouse keeper who rowed across stormy seas to save nine people from a sinking steamboat in 1838. The house of her birth has a small **museum** ① *T01668-214910, free,* run by the RNLI.

Farne Islands

① *(NT), trips to the islands can be made throughout the year from nearby Seahouses, T01655-721297, www.farne-islands.com, though the best 'birding' is to be had during the breeding season from May-Jul. Landings all year round on Inner Farne and Staple Island (at captain's discretion in bad weather), £13, children £9 for a 2-hr tour. Deep-sea fishing and diving also available. Contact the TIC near the pier T01655-721099 for other operators.*
These bare islands, beloved of birds and hermits, are one of the few places in the world where visitors can get so close to such a variety of breeding seabirds. As many as 28 species crowd on to the inhospitable rocks some 4 miles off the mainland, their numbers including an estimated 70,000 puffins, half a million fulmar as well as 3000-odd grey seals.

Guillemots, razorbills, cormorants and shags jostle for space with oyster catchers and eider duck, known locally as Cuddy duck, after St Cuthbert who spent his dying days here in 687. A chapel commemorates the community of monks who lived here until Henry VIII's Dissolution when the tower on the island was briefly used as a government fort.

Lindisfarne

Low-lying **Holy Island** is a strange mixture: the beautiful isolated setting, the picturesque ruins of the priory and the island's legacy of inspired artistry sit at odds with the concerned, almost apologetic air and limp handshake characteristic of contemporary Christianity and the inevitable tourist trappings. Linger a while, however, and wander round when the crowds return to the mainland with the high tide and the island's graceful inspiration may return.

St Aidan established the first community here in the seventh century hoping that the isolated position would provide protection and inspiration for his monks. Invited by King Oswald of Northumbria, he arrived from Iona in AD 635 making the island a base for active conversion of first the northeast and then farther afield. It became a place of considerable scholarship, encouraging literacy and a flourishing of the arts. The Benedictine monks of Lindisfarne produced wonderful illuminated texts of which the Lindisfarne Gospels, with their interlaced patterns of intricate birds and animals are the most outstandingly beautiful. Dedicated to St Cuthbert, the island's most famous hermit and reluctant abbot, they left with the monks who feared renewed attack in AD 875 and are now in the British Museum.

The **priory** ① *T01289-389200, www.lindisfarne.org.uk, daily 1000-1600, Apr-Sep 1000-1800, Oct 1000-1700, £5.20, children (5-15 years) £3.10,* whose splendid Romanesque ruins stand today, was built in the late 11th century and run by a handful of monks from Durham as a branch house until 1537. The nave of the church is particularly impressive with the stark outline of its one remaining arch, monumental columns and towering west window. The **visitor centre** ① *T01289-389004, Apr-Oct daily 1200-2000 (see website for tidal variations), £3, children (5-15 years) £1,* has a strong display and good introduction to the island's history while the 12th-century Parish Church of St Mary is also well worth a visit. Lindisfarne **castle**, largely built with stone from the abandoned priory in 1550, followed the local pattern of brief active service and lengthy decline until it was restored by Lutyens in 1903. It has a small walled garden by Gertrude Jekyll.

Berwick-upon-Tweed → *For listings, see pages 88-91.*

Berwick's graceful bridges and elegant high street belie its tempestuous border past, at the height of which the town changed hands between Scots and English no less than 13 times, making it apparently second only to Jerusalem as the most fought over city worldwide. Its famous walls have stood the test of time, however, and the oldest of the three bridges, finished in 1624, was certainly built with law and order in mind. A traveller in 1799 remarked, "The sixth pillar separates Berwick from the county of Durham. The battlements at this pillar, higher than the others, are always covered with sods as a guide to constables and others in the execution of warrants for the apprehension of delinquents." Walking across today you may be hissed at by a swan dallying on the River Tweed but otherwise passage should be uneventful, leaving you to enjoy the fine views and the prospect of a warm welcome on the other side.

Arriving in Berwick-upon-Tweed

Getting there The A1 runs up the coast from Alnwick (30 minutes) and the south, passing through Berwick on its way to Edinburgh (one hour). The A6105 takes you east to Kelso and Jedburgh. Intercity **train** services on the mainline Edinburgh (one hour) to London (4½ hours) route stop frequently; local services are good to the north and south but you are poorly served if you're coming from Carlisle and the west. **National Express** ① *T08705-808080, www.nationalexpress.co.uk*, runs coaches from London (10 hours), which also call at Newcastle (two hours) and Alnwick, before heading north to Edinburgh (1½ hours).

Getting around Arriva ① *T0191-212 3000, www.arrivabus.co.uk*, runs local services to the south. Cycling is very popular with cycle routes in abundance along the flattish coast.

Tourist information Berwick TIC ① *106 Marygate, T01670-622155, www.visitberwick.com; Easter-Oct Mon-Sat 1000-1700, May-Sep also open Sun 1100-1500; Oct-Easter Mon-Sat 1000-1600*. The website www.ford-and-etal.co.uk has useful local information.

Places in Berwick-up-Tweed

Though nothing remains of the medieval walls begun by Edward II, the town's fine Elizabethan **walls** ① *1½-hr guided tours leave from the TIC Easter-Sep Mon-Fri at 1000, 1145 and 1400; to check tours are running call T07960-062005*, were the most sophisticated that the 16th century could muster, built to an Italian design with protection from light artillery and gunfire in mind. However, as the Border Wars gradually became less ferocious, little dent was made in the 12-ft-thick walls and you can still walk almost all the way round (45 minutes). The medieval castle faired less well, though more from builders than soldiers, for the Border Bridge, the Parish Church and the Barracks are all built with its stone and it was finally demolished to make way for the 19th-century railway station.

The **Barracks** ① *(EH), T01289-304493, daily 1000-1600 (1700, Oct, 1800 Apr-Sep), closed Mon-Tue Nov-Mar, £3.90, children (5-15 years) £2.30*, designed by Vanbrugh, were the first purpose-built in England in answer to the people's protests at having scolders billeted on them. They now house a number of exhibitions including the Berwick Borough Art Gallery which includes paintings by Degas and Japanese 'Arita' pottery on loan from the Burrell collection in Glasgow.

Around Berwick

The rich, fertile countryside surrounding the town is worth exploring. It makes a modest contribution to the county's castle tally with **Norham** ① *(EH), T01289-382329*, overlooking the Tweed 6 miles to the west, and a smaller 14th-century number in the pretty village of **Etal** ① *(EH), T01890-820332*, 12 miles south. Between the two, **Heatherslaw** is notable for its unusually healthy mixture of the industrial and agricultural: the **Light Railway** ① *Ford Forge, T01890-820244, www.heatherslawlightrailway.co.uk, £6.50, children £4, trains run Apr-Oct on the hour 1100-1500, returning on the half hour from Etal*, carries children and dedicated enthusiasts, while the restored **Heatherslaw Corn Mill** on the River Till still churns out flour for delicious cakes and scones. **Lady Waterford Hall** ① *T07790-457580, www.ford-and-etal.co.uk/lady-waterford-hall, Mar-Nov daily 1100-1600, £2.50*, in Ford has a remarkable schoolhouse commissioned by an enlightened Victorian marchioness, Louisa Anne, decorated with Biblical murals, featuring local people, flora and fauna.

Central Northumberland → *For listings, see pages 88-91.*

Some of the most dramatic and beautiful moorland in the country stretches unspoilt from Hadrian's Wall in the south to the wide expanse of Kielder Water and the prominent peak of The Cheviot in the north. The return to less intense farming over the past 20 years has allowed many of the faltering species of wild flowers to return to strength, speckling the hillside with colour in May and June. The walking is exhilarating and inspiring whether you tackle the challenges of the famed Pennine Way or opt for something more gentle around Wooler or Rothbury. The paths are well-kept and clearly signed but a large scale Landranger Map or one of the more detailed walking guides is indispensable for a longer tramp. For the indoor bound, Chillingham and Cragside are well worth a visit, their wonderful gardens offering nature close at hand rather than the wilder scenery elsewhere.

Arriving in Central Northumberland
Getting there The A69 runs east–west along the south side of the park while the A697 borders the east going up to Wooler from Morpeth and the A68 comes from Jedburgh and the north. Minor B roads criss-cross the park but look out for the signs indicating military or MOD activity. Bus services are limited although the **National Express** ① *T08705-808080, www.nationalexpress.co.uk*, coach from Newcastle to Edinburgh runs twice a day with stops at Otterburn, Byrness, Jedburgh and Melrose.

Getting around Walking is highly recommended for those without transport as the scenery is unparalleled and long waits likely at the infrequent bus stops. However, local services include the postbus from Hexham to Bellingham, and **Arriva** ① *T0191-212 3000, www.arrivabus.co.uk*, service 880. There's also a service from Newcastle to Rothbury via Morpeth once a day.

Tourist information Ingram National Park **TIC** ① *T01665-578248*. **Rothbury TIC** ① *T01669-620887, www.visit-rothbury.co.uk*. **Otterburn TIC** ① *T01830-520093*. **Wooler TIC** ① *Cheviot Centre, Padgepool Place, T01668-282123, www.wooler.org.uk/visitor*. Also useful are the websites www.visitkielder.org and www.ingrambreamishvalley.co.uk.

National Park
Nearly 400 square miles of empty moorland, bog and rushing water make up the park, lying in isolated splendour on both sides of the border. Contested and viciously fought over in the Middle Ages, few villages prospered and those inhabitants who did not leave tended towards the more hospitable and easily defendable lowland areas. Aspiring romantics and the outward bound will find inspiration and challenges a plenty. The **Pennine Way** ① *www.thepennineway.co.uk, includes details of accommodation and luggage taxi*, follows the border south from Kirk Yetholm, skirting the summit of The Cheviot, turning south at Byrness and proceeding down through Bellingham to Hadrian's Wall. **St Cuthbert's Way** ① *www.stcuthbertsway.net*, follows the monk's 65-mile journey from Melrose Abbey in Scotland to Holy Island. For the less steely limbed, the two-hour walk from **Bellingham to Hareshaw Linn** has wonderful views as does the walk up to

Yavering Bell from Wooler while getting to the top of **The Cheviot** and back will take about four hours all in, but do check the latest weather forecast with Wooler TIC as low cloud and mist swoop down with unexpected speed.

The beautiful country around the wide open expanse of **Kielder Water** can seem bleak and austere in poor weather and is prone to intense midge activity from May to September making walks tough going unless there is a stiff wind or copious repellent to hand. The **Border Forest Park**, however, breaks up the moorland and offers riding as well as pleasing variety to the eye and as the most capacious man-made lake in Europe, the Water itself has the full range of fishing, boating, and other watersports available at **Leaplish Waterside Park** ① *T01434-250312, www.kielder.org.*

Bellingham is a pretty town standing on the North Tyne river and makes a good base for touring the surrounding country. You'll find thorough descriptions of good walks, and cheap guides for sale, at **Shepherds Walks** ① *T01670-774675, www.shepherdswalks.co.uk*, while **Birdwatch Northumbria** ① *T07594 592684, www.birdwatchnorthumbria.co.uk*, arranges birding for the novice watcher. The post-walk bath will undoubtedly benefit from the plant oils and organic herbs that go into the handmade goodies from the **Bellingham Soap Company** ① *T01434-681881, www.workingwithnature.co.uk.* The 12th-century **church** here is particularly fine with its stone roof consisting of hexagonal ribs overlaid with stone slabs. Medievalists may want to visit the **Percy Cross Memorial** commemorating the Battle of Otterburn (1338) where Harry Hotspur fought a moonlit battle against a Scots raiding party led by Earl Douglas.

To the east, **Rothbury** is unremarkable except for the Victorian mansion of **Cragside** ① *(NT), T01669-620333, Apr-Oct 1030-1900, house only in the afternoon, closed Sun*, built by the pioneering engineer Lord Armstrong who used it as a place to test his engineering theories, giving the house a worldwide first in the hydro-electric light stakes. The Terraced Garden contains an Orchard House and restored 19th-century clock tower.

Wooler is a good base for walking but otherwise unrewarding although **Chillingham Castle** ① *T01668-215359, www.chillingham-castle.com, Easter-Nov Sun-Fri 1200-1700, £9, children (5-15 years) £5*, to the southeast is delightful. Dating from the 12th century, it has been in the hands of the Grey family since 1245 and been lovingly and imaginatively restored by its current owners. An impressive, eclectic collection complements garden, state rooms, dungeons and torture chamber. The handsome **Chillingham Wild Cattle** ① *T01668-215250, www.chillinghamwildcattle.com, Mar-Nov Mon-Fri tours on the hour 1000-1600, Sun tours at 1000, 1100 and 1200 only, £12, children (5-15 years) £5*, roam in the park where they have done so for the past 700 years, isolated from other herds and rarely touched by human hand. Their remarkable endurance and nobility may be due to the fact that the fittest and strongest bull becomes 'King' and the leader of the herd. He remains so for just as long as no other bull can successfully challenge him in combat, and has the pleasure of siring all the calves that are born, thus ensuring only the best available blood is carried forward. Winner, as they say, takes all.

Northumberland listings

For hotel and restaurant price codes, and other relevant information, see pages 9-12.

◯ Where to stay

Alnwick and the coast *p81*
£££ The Lindisfarne Hotel, T01289-389273, http://thelindisfarnehotel.co.uk. The one to go for if you want to stay on Lindisfarne itself.

£££ Warkworth House Hotel, Bridge St, Warkworth, T01665-711276, www.warkworthhousehotel.co.uk. Comfortable and welcoming with contemporary decor and a relaxed atmosphere. Restaurant attached.

£££ Waren House Hotel, Budle Bay, T01668-214581, www.warenhouse hotel.co.uk. In a tranquil setting with views out to sea, this country house hotel offers 15 slightly old-fashioned rooms and a 5-course *table d'hôte* dinner menu.

££ Blue Bell, Market Place, Belford, T01668-213543, www.bluebellhotel.com. Less grand but welcoming and comfortable. Handy for Holy Island and the Farne Islands without being in Seahouses, which is a large bonus.

££ Schooner Hotel, Alnmouth, T01665-830216, www.theschoonerhotel.co.uk. 17th-century coaching inn with smart comfortable rooms and a hospitable atmosphere, complete with ghosts.

££ The White Swan, Bondgate Within, Alnwick, T01665-602109, www.classiclodges.co.uk/the_white_swan_hotel_alnwick. The dining room here has been kitted out with the ceiling, stained glass and panelling from the *Titanic's* sister ship, the *Olympic* though the rooms upstairs are very much *au style touristique*.

££-£ The Georgian Guest House, Hotspur St, Alnwick, T01665-602398, www.georgianguesthouse.co.uk. Very good-value accommodation close to the castle.

Self-catering
Holiday cottages available for week bookings in summer, weekends Nov to mid-Mar from the **Duke of Northumberland's Estate Office**, T01665-510777, www.northumberlandestates.co.uk.
Burton Hall, Bamburgh, T01668-214213, www.burtonhall.co.uk. Self-catering cottages.

Berwick-upon-Tweed *p84*
£££ Northumbrian House, 7 Ravensdowne, T01289-309503 www.northumbrian house.co.uk. Grade II listed building in the centre of town that has been restored into a 5-star B&B. 3 spacious rooms with original features and period furniture.

£££-££ Marshall Meadows Country House Hotel, just outside Berwick, T01289-331133, www.marshallmeadowshotel.co.uk. Caters to the well-heeled with a Victorian manor house, croquet lawn and fishing. Restaurant and bar.

££ The Cobbledyard Hotel, 40 Walkergate, T01289-308407, www.cobbledyard hotel.com. Modest family-friendly hotel in the town centre.

££ Ladythorne House, Cheswick, T01289-387382, www.ladythornehouse.co.uk. Elegant listed Georgian house dating back to 1721. Now a stylish B&B option.

££ Queens Head Hotel, 6 Sandgate, T01289-307852, www.queensheadberwick.co.uk. 6 en suite rooms with power showers and Wi-Fi. Decent restaurant attached.

£ Dewar's Lane Granary YHA, Dewar's Lane, T0845-371 9676, www.yha.org.uk/hostel/berwick. In a 240-year-old restored former granary, this 'art' hostel has loads of period features and is in a great location on the quayside.

Self-catering

Ford & Etal Estate, T01890-820647
www.ford-and-etal.co.uk. Various B&B and self-catering options across the Ford and Etal area.
Mill Lane Apartments, 2 Palace St East,
Berwick, T01289-304492. Self-catering
apartments for rent.

Central Northumberland p86

£££ Otterburn Castle Hotel, T01830-
520620, www.otterburncastle.com. This grand
old country house set in a 32-ha estate pulls
out all the stops. With 17 bedrooms, all with
Wi-Fi, it's known for its restaurant and bistro.
£££ The Percy Arms Hotel, Otterburn,
T01830-520261, www.thepercyarms.co.uk.
An old-fashioned charming hotel on the edge
of the national park, with 27 well-appointed
rooms and well-deserved reputation for
its food.
££ Bridgeford Farm, Bellingham, T01434-
220940, www.bridgefordfarmbandb.co.uk.
A working farm with a double or twin looking
out across the large garden to the Tyne.
££ Dunns Houses, Bellingham,
T01830-520677, www.northumberland
farmholidays.co.uk. Farmhouse B&B on a
privately owned estate with secluded
gardens. Pets welcome, stable facilities
for horses and has fishing.
££ Lee Farm B&B, near Rothbury,
T01665-570257, www.leefarm.co.uk. Friendly
B&B on a working farm with a lounge and sun
room for relaxing and soaking up the view.
££ Riverdale Hall Country House Hotel,
Bellingham, near Hexham, T01434-220254,
www.riverdalehallhotel.co.uk. Attractive
rooms with a good fish and game restaurant.
Self-catering also a possibility.
££ Tankerville Arms Hotel, Cottage Rd,
Wooler, T01668-281581, www.tanker
villehotel.co.uk. A 17th-century coaching inn
with 16 en suite rooms and a 2-bed
gardenhouse. The elegant **Cheviot
Restaurant** looks out over the gardens.

Self-catering

Chillingham Castle, T01668-215359,
www.chillingham-castle.com. If you want to
indulge in a bit of medieval fancy then book
a suite here.
The New Moorhouse, T01665-574638,
www.newmoorhouse.co.uk. A decidedly
cosy option.
Ridd Cottage, sleeps 6 from £500 a week
and has been well-kitted out, T0191-2533714,
www.northumberlandcottageholidays.co.uk.

❷ Restaurants

Alnwick and the coast p81

£££ Gray's Restaurant, Waren House
Hotel, Budle Bay, T01668-214581,
www.warenhousehotel.co.uk. Upmarket
with modern Northumbrian cuisine.
£36.50 per person.
££ Bailey's Bar and Restaurant, Royal
Victoria Hotel, Bamburgh, T01668-214431,
www.victoriahotel.net. High-quality local
food served in a smart new environment.
££ Blue Bell, Market Place, Belford,
T01668-213543, www.bluebellhotel.com.
Offers good bar food as well as à la carte.
££ Lilburns, Paikes St, between the Market
Place and Bondgate Within, Alnwick,
T01665-603444, www.lilburns.co.uk.
Varied menu with daily specials and
plenty of veggie options.
££-£ Di Sopra Ristorante, 9-13
Bondgate Within, Alnwick, T01665 606 540,
http://disopra-alnwick.co.uk. Smart
restaurant opened in 2012 using
authentic Italian recipes.
£ The Art House Restaurant, 14
Bondgate Within, Alnwick, T01665-602607,
www.arthouserestaurant.com. Seasonal
menu, relaxed family atmosphere.
£ Carlo's Fish & Chip Restaurant,
7-9 Market St, Alnwick, T01665-602787,
www.carlosfishandchips.co.uk. Eat in
or takeaway.

£ The Ship Inn, Low Newton by the Sea, T01665-576262, www.shipinnnewton.co.uk. In a delightful setting, this is a good stop off for coastal walkers and beachcombers.

Berwick-upon-Tweed *p84*

££ El Taperio, 52 Bridge St, T01289-309533, Authentic Spanish and Moroccan food including tapas, tagines, paellas and other tasty dishes. Also serves coffee and cake during the day.

££-£ Meadow House, North Rd, T01289 304173, www.meadow-house.co.uk. Traditional country pub a mile from the Scottish border serving proper pub grub.

£ Barrels Ale House, Bridge St, T01289-308013. Good, no-frills menu.

£ Maltings Kitchen, Eastern Lane, T01289 309 333 http://www.maltingsberwick.co.uk. Offers a pre-theatre supper or simple food to enjoy in relaxed arty environment looking out over Berwick and the Tweed.

£ The Market Shop, High St. Great if the sun is shining and you fancy a picnic.

Central Northumberland *p86*

Most of the villages in the area sport at least one if not 2 pubs with food improving steadily albeit from a lowly threshold. As elsewhere in the county, gourmets should head for the smarter hotels (see above) or pack rocket and parmesan with their wellies.

££ Chatto's Restaurant, The Blackcock Inn, Falstone, T01434-240200, www.black cockinn.co.uk. Country pub grub that will stoke you up for walking or wind you down in the evening.

££ The Cheviot Hotel, Bellingham, T01434-220696, www.thecheviothotel.co.uk. Recently refurbished and perfect for a hearty meal.

££ The Coquet Vale Hotel, Rothbury, T01669-620305, www.coquetvale.co.uk. Very popular Italian-style restaurant offering good filling fare.

⊙ Entertainment

Alnwick and the coast *p81*
Alnwick Playhouse, Bondgate Without, T01665-510785, www.alnwickplay house.co.uk. Has a variety of performances, good concerts, interesting exhibitions of local work and panto in season.

Berwick-upon-Tweed *p84*
The website www.visitberwick.co.uk has comprehensive listings for the area as does the local press.

Dewar's Lane Gallery, Dewar's Lane. Based in the recently restored 6-storey grade II listed granary building, with an exhibition space, heritage centre, bistro and youth hostel. See the Maltings Theatre website for listings or ask at the TIC.

The Maltings Theatre and Cinema, Eastern Lane, T01289-330999, www.maltingsberwick.co.uk. Has an eclectic mix of film, drama, music and art exhibitions, as well as a restaurant and bar.

Watchtower Gallery, www.berwickwatch tower.com. Creative centre for music and the arts in the former baronial watchtower. With a permanent display of paintings by the late Ian Stephenson RA, as well as regular exhibitions, concerts and performances.

⊙ Festivals

Alnwick and the coast *p81*
Jun Alnwick Fair The week-long festival begins on the last Sun.

Aug The Alnwick International Music Festival, www.alnwickmusicfestival.com, features traditional musicians and folk dancers from around the world and begins on the 1st Sat

Nov The Northumberland Gathering, www.northumbriana.org.uk/gathering, a day of traditional music competitions and events is held.

Berwick-upon-Tweed *p84*

Aug Given the town's history, the **Berwick Military Tattoo**, www.berwickmilitary tattoo.co.uk, in the last weekend in Aug is the chief highlight.

▲ What to do

Alnwick and the coast *p81*
Fishing

Fishermen will find inspiration at **The House of Hardy**, 4 miles to the south on the A1, T01665-510027, www.hardyfishing.com/ en-gb/home, and, appropriately kitted out, will find fly, sea and coarse fishing available.

Mon-Sat 0900-1700. The River Aln has some fishing while the River Coquet to the south is stocked and managed by the **Northumberland Anglers Federation**, T01670-787663, www.northumbrian anglersfed.co.uk.

Walking

Walkers not tempted by the bigger challenges of **The Cheviot** and surrounding hills should head for **Hulne Park**, www.northumberlandestates.co.uk/walks_ hulnepark.php, on the outskirts of town.

Contents

Footnotes

Index

Titles available in the Footprint *Focus* range

Latin America	UK RRP	US RRP
Bahia & Salvador	£7.99	$11.95
Brazilian Amazon	£7.99	$11.95
Brazilian Pantanal	£6.99	$9.95
Buenos Aires & Pampas	£7.99	$11.95
Cartagena & Caribbean Coast	£7.99	$11.95
Costa Rica	£8.99	$12.95
Cuzco, La Paz & Lake Titicaca	£8.99	$12.95
El Salvador	£5.99	$8.95
Guadalajara & Pacific Coast	£6.99	$9.95
Guatemala	£8.99	$12.95
Guyana, Guyane & Suriname	£5.99	$8.95
Havana	£6.99	$9.95
Honduras	£7.99	$11.95
Nicaragua	£7.99	$11.95
Northeast Argentina & Uruguay	£8.99	$12.95
Paraguay	£5.99	$8.95
Quito & Galápagos Islands	£7.99	$11.95
Recife & Northeast Brazil	£7.99	$11.95
Rio de Janeiro	£8.99	$12.95
São Paulo	£5.99	$8.95
Uruguay	£6.99	$9.95
Venezuela	£8.99	$12.95
Yucatán Peninsula	£6.99	$9.95

Asia	UK RRP	US RRP
Angkor Wat	£5.99	$8.95
Bali & Lombok	£8.99	$12.95
Chennai & Tamil Nadu	£8.99	$12.95
Chiang Mai & Northern Thailand	£7.99	$11.95
Goa	£6.99	$9.95
Gulf of Thailand	£8.99	$12.95
Hanoi & Northern Vietnam	£8.99	$12.95
Ho Chi Minh City & Mekong Delta	£7.99	$11.95
Java	£7.99	$11.95
Kerala	£7.99	$11.95
Kolkata & West Bengal	£5.99	$8.95
Mumbai & Gujarat	£8.99	$12.95

Africa & Middle East	UK RRP	US RRP
Beirut	£6.99	$9.95
Cairo & Nile Delta	£8.99	$12.95
Damascus	£5.99	$8.95
Durban & KwaZulu Natal	£8.99	$12.95
Fès & Northern Morocco	£8.99	$12.95
Jerusalem	£8.99	$12.95
Johannesburg & Kruger National Park	£7.99	$11.95
Kenya's Beaches	£8.99	$12.95
Kilimanjaro & Northern Tanzania	£8.99	$12.95
Luxor to Aswan	£8.99	$12.95
Nairobi & Rift Valley	£7.99	$11.95
Red Sea & Sinai	£7.99	$11.95
Zanzibar & Pemba	£7.99	$11.95

Europe	UK RRP	US RRP
Bilbao & Basque Region	£6.99	$9.95
Brittany West Coast	£7.99	$11.95
Cádiz & Costa de la Luz	£6.99	$9.95
Granada & Sierra Nevada	£6.99	$9.95
Languedoc: Carcassonne to Montpellier	£7.99	$11.95
Málaga	£5.99	$8.95
Marseille & Western Provence	£7.99	$11.95
Orkney & Shetland Islands	£5.99	$8.95
Santander & Picos de Europa	£7.99	$11.95
Sardinia: Alghero & the North	£7.99	$11.95
Sardinia: Cagliari & the South	£7.99	$11.95
Seville	£5.99	$8.95
Sicily: Palermo & the Northwest	£7.99	$11.95
Sicily: Catania & the Southeast	£7.99	$11.95
Siena & Southern Tuscany	£7.99	$11.95
Sorrento, Capri & Amalfi Coast	£6.99	$9.95
Skye & Outer Hebrides	£6.99	$9.95
Verona & Lake Garda	£7.99	$11.95

North America	UK RRP	US RRP
Vancouver & Rockies	£8.99	$12.95

Australasia	UK RRP	US RRP
Brisbane & Queensland	£8.99	$12.95
Perth	£7.99	$11.95

For the latest books, e-books and a wealth of travel information, visit us at:
www.footprinttravelguides.com.

 footprinttravelguides.com

Join us on facebook for the latest travel news, product releases, offers and amazing competitions:
www.facebook.com/footprintbooks.